Stronger

INCREASE YOUR PERSONAL DEPTH AND WISDOM

VOLUME 1

Stronger: Increase Your Personal Depth and Wisdom

published by Kidmin Nation

edited by Tina Houser

copyright ©2019

ISBN: 978-1-950718-02-3

cover design by Vanessa Mendozzi

CONTENTS

INTRODUCTION

MOST OF THE TIME, using the word *strong* to describe someone is a compliment. Even being referred to as "strong-willed" can make you feel good about yourself. My mind moves toward *being confident in a particular area* when I contemplate being strong—having strength in that area.

In children's ministry there's always something to learn. Simply staying in that zone where you're constantly evaluating new resources, new methods, new activities contributes to feeling strong, like you're on top of what's happening in this ministry field. But there's more to it than being able to write a review of each company's line of curriculum, creating a new environment, or putting together a new game. Spiritually, emotionally, socially, and physically, when you feel strong, you envision yourself standing a little taller and taking a deeper breath. You're more than managing. You've got this!

If you ask someone what would make them feel stronger, their answer would probably be something that they currently feel is lacking a bit. Taking steps toward strengthening one area can have a ripple effect and actually make you feel stronger in subsequent areas. If your answer to that question is, "I feel stronger when I'm managing my health"; then, exercising, eating correctly, drinking lots of water, and getting plenty of rest are actions you can take to accomplish that. When you physically feel good, though, it shows up in an increased ability: to deal with conflict (which makes you feel stronger), to put fear in your back pocket (which makes you feel more confident and stronger), or to deal with the pain of hurtful comments (which makes you feel what? Stronger!).

There's a huge array of answers to that question, depending on where you find yourself at the present time. Notice, I said *present* time. That's because it changes. When you feel deplet-ed in one area, you focus your thoughts on feeling stronger in that area. What you are lacking in your present situation and condition seems to take over the way you process many other areas. But, this doesn't have to be a gloomy scenario!

Can you imagine yourself being stronger when you pursue more education? Then, there's something you can do about that. Stop imagining being strong and take one step toward identifying yourself as someone who values continual learn-ing. Sign up for a church history course. Go on a guided tour of the Holy Lands and walk where Jesus walked. Enroll in seminary. Get involved in a group who dives deep into the Scripture. If that's where you find yourself, I bet just reading those options got your heart beating a little faster.

If you find yourself stretched thin and feeling overwhelmed because you're involved in too many activities and ministries, you probably agree that you would feel stronger if you learned how to say *no*. It's a matter of saying yes to the right things— the things that God has called you to. The first thing you need to master is the ability to actually put your lips together and pronounce the word, "No." Look in the mirror and see what it looks like. Did you think it was even possible?

I love the church. I love being part of a lot of different activ-ities. I want every ministry to succeed. And, I'm actually pret-ty good at a lot of things. Those four statements make it even harder to say *no*. For example, I couldn't say *no* when asked to be part of the outreach planning committee. My brain imme-diately went to family-oriented community-related ways to minister, and that got me excited. Not so with the rest of the committee. They envisioned a women's conference that would meet the needs of women who struggled with self-worth and needed a spiritual boost. That was a fabulous idea! But wom-en's ministry is not, and never has been, my cup of tea. (In my own defense, it goes back to my days as a young pastor's wife. Every women's event I attended was an opportunity for pastors' wives to complain about how terrible their church treated them. I could not identify and didn't want to be involved in that kind of environment. That's my excuse and I'm sticking with it.) The women's conference was a huge amount of work, took a lot of time, and honestly, my heart wasn't in it. It was my own fault. I couldn't face the person asking me and form the word *no*. I eventually was able to make that little circle with my mouth and stepped away from that obligation. Instead, I focused on what God called me to do—kids! And, I am stronger for it and the church is better off.

What is it that would make you feel *STRONGer*... as a leader? As a parent? As a friend? As a person on this journey called life? Identify it and then take one step toward becoming *STRONGer*. Your ultimate strength comes from the Lord, and He wants you to feel fulfilled. I cherish the beautiful message in Isaiah 41:10 (NIV), *"So do not fear, for I am with you; do not be dismayed, for I am your God. I will strengthen you and help you; I will uphold you with my righteous right hand."*

To become stronger physically, you need to be committed as you stretch your muscles to a new level. The same is true for being stronger emotionally, socially, and spiritually—be committed and stretch yourself. God desires for you to be your strongest self. He will *"strengthen you and help you."* Now go... be *STRONGer*.

In His incredible joy,

tina!

chapter 1

LOST AND FOUND AND DODGEBALL

*You are stronger when you're
reminded of your calling.*

BY KRISSY RICHARDSON

I DIDN'T EVEN KNOW what I had lost.

There I was, standing in the middle of the gym surrounded by preteens with dodgeballs—this would be the classic movie time-freeze-epiphany moment. The cameras would pan around as everything freezes and blurs, and you'd see the epiphany crystallize on the main actor's face. Instead, I was hit by eight dodgeballs at once and treated to a chorus of delighted laughter as the preteens scattered.

I got here out of necessity: 12 kids, mostly boys, our biggest class ever, moving into 4ᵗʰ grade by September. I was afraid that I'd watch them get bored and disruptive or slowly stop coming to church, like had happened with too many kids in the past. They were too old to be treated like the rest of the kids, too young to be sent up to the teen world. Something needed to be done! So, after eight months of learning about how pre-teens work and coming up with a plan, our first preteen meet-up concluded with dodgeball. Twenty minutes later when they were all gone, I collapsed on the floor of my classroom, ex-hausted but invigorated, with tears in my eyes and my breath catching in my chest.

I'd lost something.

All that time and energy spent on building the preteen min-istry came out of genuine love for the kids and a desire to serve God. But all that time, I was serving on auto pilot. I saw a need and, capable person that I am, I handled it. I'd been doing in other areas of ministry, too. Week after week I was faithfully teaching, cutting out flannelgraph pieces, thanking volun-teers, planning events, and attending meetings. Had I lost touch with God? No. Had I stopped loving the kids? Not one bit. But I had lost something so slowly, piece by piece, that I didn't even know it was gone.

A simple game of dodgeball brought it all into focus: I'd lost sight of my calling. I'd forgotten the clear, loud voice, of so many years ago saying, "Serve the little ones, find the lost with-in the church, stand with the families." Along with losing sight of my calling, I'd lost the joy that comes from the privilege of serving our wonderful God. I was heartbroken and ashamed. How could I have lost something so important? How could I have lost it while still serving faithfully?

Before going any further, take a few minutes to humbly re-flect on where you stand today. Pray and ask God to reveal the true state of your heart and mind in relation to your calling. It might not be as easy to discern as you think. Thankfully, you serve a faithful God who will be there if you are seeking Him. Here's a few questions to help you in the process:

- Has ministry started to feel like an obligation or just part of the routine?
- Are you weary or exhausted, and not in a good way?
- Do you feel defeated or uninspired?
- Have you been tempted to start things in your ministry simply because you saw it working for another ministry/ church?
- Do you find yourself reluctant to do work you once enjoyed?
- Have you stopped having fun with your kids and your team?
- Do you feel paralyzed by indecision of what to do next in your ministry?

Have you lost sight of your calling? Answering *yes* to any of the above is an indication that something is wrong. There are two ways you can lose sight of your calling: (1) longing for someone else's ministry or (2) by losing the joy in your own. Most of the time, it's a combination of the two or one led to the other. Maybe it fell away, little by little, so gradually that you hadn't even noticed. Or maybe you can point to the moment when your calling stopped being joyful and became just another part of your day. No matter how it happened, you don't have to stay there. God hasn't changed. He has called you to great things! Let's get started on the hard work of getting back to a place where you can serve God joyfully in the full knowledge of your calling. You will be stronger there.

Find what you've been missing—assurance of who you are in Christ. After I recognized what I'd lost, the first thing I needed to do was repent and ask God for forgiveness over the choices that had led me to this place. The very next thing I needed to do was grieve what had been lost. Grief is a normal part of moving forward after a loss. Try to avoid it, and you're hurting yourself (and possibly others) down the road. It's a big deal to have a calling on your life, hear it clearly, and act on it! And that means that it's a sad thing to lose sight of too. Take the time you need to grieve what was lost and the mistakes you've made. As you do so, remember that you're more than the things you've lost... even more than the calling on your life.

Isaiah 43:1-4 (NLT) says:

"But now, O Jacob, listen to the Lord who created you. O Israel, the one who formed you says, 'Do not be afraid, for I have ransomed you. I have called you by name; you are mine. When you go through deep waters, I will be with you. When you go through rivers of difficulty, you will not drown. When you walk through the fire of oppression, you will not be burned up; the flames will not consume you. For I am the Lord, your God, the Holy One of Israel, your Savior. I gave Egypt as a ransom for your freedom; I gave Ethiopia and Seba in your place. Others were given in exchange for you. I traded their lives for yours because you are precious to me. You are honored, and I love you.'"

You have not only been called; you belong to God. He wants you. You are precious to Him. He loves you. And through all this upheaval and loss, He is there and will not leave you. You are stronger when you know who you are and whose you are.

FIND WHAT YOU'VE BEEN MISSING: GO BACK IN TIME

When you're done grieving, it's time to go back and find your calling again. Whether you've fallen into the trap of wanting the ministry someone else has, or you've lost the joy in your calling, or both, this is an important step. You can't undo what has been done, but you can think back on a time before this loss. Prayerfully, look back to the time when you first felt truly called into ministry. Ask God to sharpen that memory for you.

When was that calling? Where were you? Who were the people God called you to love? How did you know that this was God's call on your life? What made you excited about that call on your life? Stay in that moment for a while. Let the excitement, anticipation, and joy of that moment wash over you again.

When you're ready, the next step is to go back to the last thing you absolutely know God called you to. If you've been in ministry for a long time, this might be different than that first calling. My father-in-law, a pastor of more then 40 years, often says, "When you aren't sure what to do next, go back to the last thing you know God told you to do." His wisdom applies to your calling as well. If you've lost sight of your calling, you've probably been on auto-pilot for too long. What was the last thing you clearly remember God calling you to? Where were you? Was it different than your first call to ministry? What made you excited about that call on your life? Is this still what God has called you to? Again, let that moment wash over you and begin to feel the joy like it was brand new today.

As you're looking back, remember that everyone's calling is different. You might be called to missions near or far, pre-schoolers or preteens, a mega church or a tiny church, music or sports. Each calling is unique and wonderful like you and the people God called you to serve. When you've lost sight of your own calling, it's easy to look around at others and want the assurance and successes they have. Suddenly, that thriving after-school program looks like the way to go. That new curriculum looks like the answer to all your problems. That church down the street has all the kids who should be coming to yours. This may seem appealing, but it's not the way to get back what was lost. Remember: Your calling is unique to you and the people you serve. Do not try to substitute someone else's calling in place of your own. This is between you and the God who called you. You are stronger when you are reminded of *your* calling.

FIND WHAT YOU'VE BEEN MISSING: BRING BACK THE JOY

While I highly recommend dodgeball with preteens, I also admit that it might not work for everyone. Dodgeball wasn't what truly restored my joy anyway. What dodgeball did was give me a reason to be in the moment with my kids, having fun and enjoying their company. It provided the spark I needed to remind me of that great calling. It had been far too long since I had simply had fun with the kids. Part of losing the joy was feeling bogged down by administration, discipline, and a long list of "have tos" instead of "get tos."

Think about a part of ministry that used to be fun for you. There's no right or wrong answer. Maybe it's dodgeball or maybe it's lesson planning. Maybe it's creating a cool environment or maybe it's holding a baby. Whatever it is, find a way to do it again. Joy cannot be created from circumstances, but it can be sparked by doing things that are truly fun and enjoyable.

If you can't think of anything that used to be fun, and you've prayed earnestly, it might be time for some outside help. Go to a trusted friend or mentor who has known you over the course of your ministry. Ask them to tell you what you love about ministry. Ask them to remind you why you started in ministry, what has kept you putting in the long hours, what used to get you all riled up in conversations about ministry. A little hint: If something gets you up on a soap box, that's probably something you're passionate about and it's likely linked to your calling somehow!

FIND WHAT YOU'VE BEEN MISSING: PROTECT THE FUTURE

Ministry is exhausting... worth it, but exhausting. When you've found yourself solidly in sight of your calling again, with joy bubbling up as you continue to serve, it's time to think about the future. Perhaps God's calling on your life has changed slightly, or you've got some work to do to set yourself and ministry back on track to where God's leading. This is a new beginning!

Chances are, that if you lost the joy in your calling, your team needs a joy-boost too. Take time over the next few weeks to remind them of who they are (and whose they are!), why they're important to your ministry, and find a meaningful way to thank them. You might consider hosting an appreciation night where you share the vision you have for the ministry moving forward. Joy is contagious and inspiring!

If you have implemented things into your ministry simply because it worked for someone else, you're going to need to examine them carefully. Not all things done for that reason are bad or need to be discontinued. That's going to be up to you to figure out with God and your team. You will want to consider having conversations with a core group of people on your team to look closely at the ministry to see what is truly in line with the vision set by the church and your calling.

The God who called you still wants you. You, faithful servant, are called by name and you are His (Isaiah 43:1). You've already done great things. Think of how much better it will be when all this hard work is done. You're stronger when you are reminded of your calling! So, what are you being called to today? How are you going to get that joy back so you can continue to serve? How are you going to inspire your team and keep that calling alive? What hard work still needs to be done? You've got this. You are strong.

Krissy Richardson has been serving in children's ministry for over 17 years, and is currently the Director of GraceKids in Warren, OR. In her spare time, she rarely plays dodgeball (that's more her husband's thing), but can often be found sitting at her sewing machine with a cup of tea while her two little girls create beautiful chaos around her.

chapter 2

35,000 DECISIONS A DAY

*You are stronger when you
include God in all decisions.*

BY COURTNEY KIRK

L IFE IS FULL of decisions. Will I hit the snooze button
again? What will I wear? Will I eat a healthy salad or
give in to a slice of pizza? Chocolate or vanilla? It has
been suggested by the scientific community that people make
nearly 35,000 decisions every single day. Most decisions are
made without even thinking about them, but others, you get
hung up on for hours, days, and even weeks. What is your decision-making matrix, whether big or small? Be honest. Is your
initial reaction to go to God?

Let's face it, in kidmin, you have a big, important job to do that involves a number of decisions. The decisions you make impact the spiritual lives of God's children as you strive to form a solid foundation on Christ. How do you get in front of children? How do you present God's message in a way they understand? How do you inspire a love for God and a desire to know Him more? These are just a few of the questions a kidmin leader wrestles with every day and you cannot, nor should you attempt to, do so without God guiding your steps.

Who has ever stopped to plan the following year with the intent of growing the ministry? How many of you began with the question of curriculum or advertising? There's nothing wrong with taking a deeper look at the curriculum or advertising to the public, but is this where you really need to start? It may be for you. For me, I went through this exercise when I started in children's ministry and found the solutions were different from the beginning to the end of the process. Did it work? Definitely! With God in the lead it was destined to be a success. My Bible class sizes doubled, the kids were consistently attending weekly, they were retaining information, and parents were incredibly supportive.

Big or small, always include God in the decisions. You may have the best of intentions and the greatest ideas, or so you think, but if God is not in support, you have a problem. He sees clearly when you cannot. *"There is a way that appears to be right, but in the end it leads to death"* (Proverbs 14:12, NIV). These are my seven steps to decision-making.

1. BEGIN WITH PRAYER.

"Ask and it will be given to you; seek and you will find; knock and the door will be opened to you" (Matthew 7:7, NIV). God is clear; you just need to ask Him and He will show you the way. Never underestimate the power of prayer. God hears your pleas, and not only that, prayer has an amazing effect on you. It directs your focus towards God.

2. CLARIFY THE ISSUE.

"Above all else, guard your heart, for everything you do flows from it" (Proverbs 4:23, NIV). Know the issue, the root concern; otherwise, you may get sidetracked and never solve the real dilemma. For instance, before you start trying to solve the issue of curriculum like I was, decide what your goal is. Mine was to get the current children who attended occasionally to become frequent, regular attendees who were learning about God. When curriculum is the issue, that's when you focus on curriculum.

3. GATHER INFORMATION.

"To answer before listening—that is folly and shame" (Proverbs 18:13, NIV). Take time to brainstorm. Get the facts and information surrounding your issue. Write everything down that comes to mind. Trust that God is at work in you.

4. OPTIONS.

"Do not conform to the pattern of this world but be transformed by the renewing of your mind. Then you will be able to test and approve what God's will is—his good, pleasing and perfect will" (Romans 12:2, NIV). Now that you have the information, you can create God-approved options. Hopefully, they are flowing at this point. Be open to the idea that your initial thought going into this may not be the best. It may not be the one God desires. What does God say about your topic? Search the scriptures looking for direct commands or examples. Remember, there is nothing new under the sun, so, chances are, there are solutions within the pages of God's Word.

4. EVALUATE.

"Suppose one of you wants to build a tower. Won't you first sit down and estimate the cost to see if you have enough money to complete it?" (Luke 14:28, NIV). Review your options and talk them over with God.

4. CHOOSE.

"Anyone who chooses to do the will of God will find out whether my teaching comes from God or whether I speak on my own" (John 7:17, NIV). After seeking God in prayer and trusting Him to lead you to a wise choice, it's time to choose. This can be exciting and scary!

5. ACT.

"We should make plans—counting on God to direct us" (Proverbs 16:9, TLB). Now it's time to follow through, letting God continue to guide you and work through you. Remember, this life is not about you; you are the hands and feet of God. Act on His behalf.

Let's look at a biblical example from 1 Samuel 23. David was a man after God's own heart. He loved God and trusted him. King Saul was out to kill David, so he was on the run. At this time in history, David led an army of misfits, men who were all in some kind of trouble.

One day David was told that the Philistines were fighting against Keilah and robbing grain from the threshing floors. David knew the facts and had clarity of the issue; he knew the real problem. He knew his options were to fight or not to fight. David had proven he was a strong and valiant warrior; however, he did not rush into battle. First, he went to God in prayer and let God guide his decision. God said to go fight the Philistines and save Keilah. But wait! David's men were afraid. David took a step back and returned to God. God told him again to fight; then David took action and succeeded because he followed God.

On a personal note, after some trial and error, I went through each of these steps over the course of several weeks to solve a problem one of my teachers was running into. I had not been overseeing the children's ministry for long when I was asked for some solutions in handling a very hyper little girl. The teacher knew that the parents were used to hearing from the school with issues and did not want to put pressure on her at church, too. She wanted the parents to feel completely comfortable continuing to bring their daughter to Bible class week after week but needed some guidance. This was something I had not yet faced, so I didn't have the answer immediately.

I went home that Sunday determined to come up with a plan. I did all kinds of research and found ideas online. I was so excited to share those with the teacher, but after weeks of testing them, none worked. What was I going to do? I realized I had not gone to God. That should have been my first step; instead, I tried to handle it on my own using earthly wisdom. There is absolutely nothing wrong with earthly wisdom; after all, God created the earth and its patterns. There is a rhyme and a reason to how the world works. Who would know better how to handle a hyper, disruptive child than the One who created her?

I went back to the drawing board. I spent a lot of time with God in prayer. Second, I clearly defined the issue. A child was hyper and disruptive causing the teacher to become frustrated and discouraged while preventing other children from learning God's Word. When I broke it down like this, I realized it was a bigger problem than I originally thought. It negatively impacted every single one of the kids in class and the teacher.

Now it was time to gather information. Thankfully, I had already done quite a bit of online research. I also checked into this little girl's family background to see if anything might be contributing to her behavior. I continued to talk to God throughout this whole process, not just step one. During my fact-gathering session, I noted that this child came from a home with one non-Christian parent and one extremely involved parent. Both worked so she spent a lot of time in school and day care. She enjoyed plenty of time on electronics when home, often playing video games with Dad. On top of it, although undiagnosed, I believe she suffered from ADHD.

I learned that these children need structure, patience, some grace, and movement.

Movement? But my classrooms were not large, nor did I need little girls in dresses running, falling, and accidentally showing things they should not. Yikes! What choices did I have? I brainstormed some more and when I put all this information together, I had a plan. I trusted God to lead me and He did! I chose to use play-dough, kinetic sand, and play foam in every lesson. Each child had their own to hold and mold throughout the lesson. Movement without needing space that I did not have.

Did it work? Absolutely! Not only did it help that one hyper little girl, but it helped every single child in that class. The teacher was thrilled and no longer dreaded teaching every week. All the kids had fun, visitors were coming into class without hesitation, and the kids were learning and retaining more than they had ever learned before. It worked so well that I expanded this to other ages and am still amazed today at how well it worked. All I did was include God in my decision. I let Him work through me. God's ways were clearly better than mine.

Not all decisions require the time and attention of these seven steps. For instance, you may be asked to lead a prayer before class begins. There are some decisions that do not take a lot of thought; however, God should still be included. How can you know that you're making little decisions God's way?

It's hard to fathom that the very same spirit that rose Jesus from the grave lives in me. Mind boggling! Why would you choose to do anything on your own when you have the Holy Spirit in you? *"God can do anything, you know, far more than you could ever imagine or guess or request in your wildest dreams! He does it not by pushing us around but by working within us, his Spirit deeply and gently within us"* (Ephesians 3:20-21, MSG). Because of this, I am stronger when I involve God in all decisions and actions, big and small, throughout the day.

The first step is intentionality. Wake up every single day with God first. *"Set your minds on things above"* (Colossians 3:20a, NIV). You may begin with a prayer, a scripture, or even a Bible study. The point is, begin with God and let Him lead you throughout the day. When you direct your thoughts towards God and His will, your decisions will reflect wisdom and godliness. This may not come naturally at first, but if you're diligent in your pursuit, it will become second nature. If you need to, set alarms to remind you to stop for a few minutes throughout the day and spend some time with God. In no time, you'll be doing it on your own.

Next, humble yourself. To be filled with the spirit, make room for the spirit. Get rid of your big head. *"God gives strength to the humble but sets himself against the proud and haughty"* (James 4:6, TLB). Let God work through you for His purpose. *"Commit to the LORD whatever you do, and he will establish your **plans"*** (Proverbs 16:3, NIV). As God's plans succeed, give Him the glory.

Imagine your children's ministry when God is always included. Imagine your attitude and peace of mind when God is constantly part of your journey. Scripture said it best, *"Depend on the Lord for strength. Always go to him for help"* (1 Chronicles 16:11, ERV.) How will you make your 35,000 decisions today?

Courtney Kirk serves as a K-5th grade Children's Ministry Coordinator. She is the founder of RaiseKidsForChrist.com, dedicated to helping those in children's ministry run more effective Bible classes through play—the way kids learn best!

chapter 3

NO PAIN, NO GAIN

*You are stronger when you
grow through spiritual disciplines.*

BY PAT CONNER

I'M NOT A MARATHON runner. Actually, I'm not any kind of a runner, but occasionally I am a marathon spectator. I enjoy the experience of standing in a crowd, cheerfully encouraging athletes or would-be athletes as they run the race set before them. As a spectator, I'm fascinated. I'm fascinated by the number of people who take on the challenge. I'm fascinated to see people of all ages and all backgrounds daring to test themselves. What preoccupies me most, however, is not what I'm seeing during the race. I am captivated by the thought of what every runner has done leading up to race day.

What I don't see is how those runners disciplined themselves to prepare for the run. I don't see the countless days they got up before dawn to run or train. I don't see the thousands of decisions they made to eat this, not that, so their bodies would be stronger. I don't see what they denied themselves so they would be strong enough to run this race. I don't see the injuries or aches they have tended and tolerated. I don't have to see those things to know they have happened. Without self-denial, without consistent training, and without pain, no runner gains the strength and endurance necessary to compete in a marathon.

For a non-runner like me, it can be difficult to see how this discipline is worth it, but it sets a great example for me in another area. Just as a runner equips himself to run a race by the discipline of physical training, so training through spiritual disciplines enables me to do life and ministry in the strength of the grace of Jesus. Paul talked about this in 1 Timothy. *"Train yourself in godliness. For the training of the body has limited benefit, but godliness is beneficial in every way, since it holds promise for the present life and also for the life to come"* (1 Timothy 4:7b-8, CSB).

Train yourself in godliness! What an exciting thought! I am able to train myself to be more like Jesus. I understand there is always a cost and very often pain in training, but what a gain! I want to be more like Him. I want to be like Jesus with my family and friends. I want to be like Jesus in my ministry. And there are things I can do to equip myself for that.

Taken as a group, these training exercises are called "spiritual disciplines." Spiritual disciplines are things you do in order to be more like Jesus. These are not attitudes or character traits, such as the fruit of the spirit. These are practices you can use as discipline that will turn into life habits. As you do that, you're cooperating with God so He can transform you. Spiritual disciplines are vitally important, not because they indicate spiritual success, but because they equip you to live in the full reality of God's strengthening work in your life. That's discipline that's worth it!

What are the spiritual disciplines? Because the Bible doesn't give a comprehensive catalog of these practices, different believers may produce different lists. A good standard to follow is that spiritual disciplines should be practices taught in the Bible as ways to become godlier. My list is not exhaustive, but I'm happy to share, in no particular order, the disciplines that are valuable in my own life.

BIBLE STUDY

I've never gotten over my utter astonishment that the God of the Universe gave us a book so we can know Him better. It's not just any book. 2 Timothy recalls that, *"All Scripture is inspired by God and is profitable for teaching, for rebuking, for correcting, for training in righteousness, so that the man of God may be complete, equipped for every good work"* (2 Timothy 3:16-17, CSB). You have a book that's designed by God to equip you for ministry. How could you not discipline yourself to spend time reading that book? In my own practice, I use different methods of Scripture reading or study. Some years I've read through the Bible. During some seasons of life, I study a particular book or research what the Bible has to say about a specific topic. Scripture reading is not the same as reading a devotional book or a book about the Bible.

Through reading and mentally understanding the words of Scripture, your mind is transformed. You become more able to follow the pattern of truth in the Bible. The words of the Bible are living words, designed by God to change you as part of His work in your life. Jen Wilkin, one of my favorite teachers, has helped me grasp how Bible study can work effectively in my life. Jen says that, too often, people think of Bible reading as a debit account, where you can put in your card and take out what you need for that day. However, it may be better to consider studying the Bible as a savings account where you make small deposits on a regular basis. These small deposits mean you can grow in your knowledge of Scripture, giving you a broader knowledge of God's Word and transforming your mind as you follow this discipline. ("A Knowing Faith" podcast, Jen Wilkin) Though lists of spiritual disciplines may vary, reading and studying the Bible is a necessary discipline for every growing believer.

MEDITATION

The practice of meditation is closely related to Bible study. The word *meditation* is connected with non-Christian practices in ways that can make meditation seem undesirable. There's a difference in the mystical practice of some religions and the practice of meditation for Christians. For some, the goal of meditation is to empty one's mind. For Christians, the goal of meditation is to fill your mind with the presence and truth of Christ. In its simplest form, meditation is the repetitious going-over of a matter in one's mind.

This is why I connect the discipline of meditation with the discipline of Bible study. If I'm repeatedly going over something in my mind, I want it to be something absolutely true. Meditation becomes a beneficial spiritual discipline when I use it to go over the Word of God or the character of God. As I spend time rehearsing who God is, my mind expands in a greater understanding of Him and my heart expands in a greater love for Him. I am training for godliness.

SOLITUDE

I can guess what you're thinking: "There's no space or time or quietness in my life for meditation." For sure, the world you live and minister in is busy and noisy and crowded and frantic. Too often the things you're repeatedly going over in your mind is your to-do lists or your worries or your pressure points. I've come to highly value solitude as a spiritual discipline. Often "solitude" is paired with "silence" as a single practice of spiritual discipline. The fact that solitude was important for Jesus convinced me that it should be important in my life as well.

The Bible clearly shows that Jesus sought solitude. This happened as He prepared to launch His earthly ministry, before He called His 12 disciples, when He was distressed, and after major periods of ministry. If the Lord pursued time alone with the Father, I want to do that, also.

For quite a while it has been my practice to plan "quiet days" a few times a year. At some stages of my life I've been able to do this in my own empty nest. At other times, I've needed to go away to a different location for a night and a day. The purpose of these days is to be quiet, putting myself in a listening posture so I can more fully connect with God. Being quiet is harder than you might think. I find myself addicted to noise and busy-ness. Perhaps you are, too. It's difficult to connect with God if you don't slow down and listen. The discipline of solitude helps to do that.

PRAYER

I love the easy give and take of talking with my close friends and family. The ability to have the same type of conversation with God is a stunning gift, and in some ways to name prayer as a discipline feels not quite right. Shouldn't prayer be so enjoyable that you rush to it? Maybe so, but still prayer must be on any list of spiritual disciplines. It must be acknowledged as a vital training exercise. Prayer does not usually come naturally or easily. Along with the disciples, you need to ask, *"Lord, teach us to pray"* Luke 11:1, CSB). The good news is that He does teach you. God meets you where you are and guides you into His way of thinking. It is often in prayer that your heart is changed and you begin to want what God wants. It is in conversation with Him that you come to know God better.

For many Christians, prayer is a routine part of each day. Prayer is simply talking with God, ideally in a two-way conversation where you listen as well as talk. I usually keep a prayer journal and follow a pattern of praise, confession, thanksgiving, intercession, and supplication. You may have a similar pattern.

Some days prayer comes easily and some days it feels like work. That's how training is! Your job is to keep on praying. In fact, your job is to learn to *"pray constantly"* (1 Thessalonians 5:17, CSB). This type of prayer that keeps you in touch with God through every part of every day is a goal of mine. I'm not there yet, but I'm in training. Prayer—your ongoing connection with your living God—is a great gift of grace as you participate in His work in your life and in the world around you.

FASTING

Fasting is definitely taught in the Bible and is often listed as one of the spiritual disciplines. Before He began His public ministry Jesus Himself spent 40 days fasting. He seems to have assumed that His followers would fast as He said to a group of them *"whenever you fast..."* (Matthew 6:16, CSB). Though fasting doesn't seem to be commanded in the Bible, it does seem to be accepted and expected.

What exactly is fasting? Fasting can be described as the practice of intentionally abstaining from some form of physical satisfaction in order to achieve a more important spiritual purpose. This definition expands the understanding of fasting as more than simply going without food. Fasting can mean giving up any type of physical pleasure for a period a time. There is more to fasting than just giving up something. You give up something *for* a spiritual purpose. The abstinence is only a means to an end. The purpose of fasting is that you turn your focus to God.

Many Christians fast routinely as a spiritual discipline. Routinely may mean one day each week. It may be once a month. Other Christians may fast during times of unique circumstances. Often people fast as part of an intercession when they pray for a deeply felt need. Sometimes I have fasted when I desperately wanted to discern God's thoughts in a particular situation. Fasting is a training exercise that teaches you to turn your eyes from the temporary and intently align yourself with God and His ways. As such, it is a valuable spiritual discipline.

SERVICE

Philippians 2 paints a clear picture of what it means to be like Jesus. *"Adopt the same attitude as that of Christ Jesus, who, existing in the form of God, did not consider equality with God as something to be exploited. Instead he emptied himself by assuming the form of a servant, taking on the likeness of humanity"* (Philippians 2:5-7, CSB). Because Jesus came to be a servant, you are to serve others as well. This discipline of service begins with a deliberate mindset of considering others more important than yourself, but it continues with a lifetime of practicing service. There is no way to be like Jesus without serving others.

I find serving in my church or even in the church world to be easy. I consider it right and a part of my calling as a minister. Serving in a church is fun to me! The truth is that the discipline, or training, part of service for me comes more in community or neighborhood service. For example, I intentionally volunteer with a local hospice company. I deliberately look for ways to serve people in my neighborhood. Service is a spiritual discipline for me when I am intentional about doing it with the attitude of Christ. The acts of service that I choose to do will be used by God to change me.

Bible study, meditation, solitude, prayer, fasting, and service are all ways I consider myself to be in training. There is no doubt that I am stronger spiritually when I am consistently practicing these spiritual disciplines. It is not that I'm making myself be like Jesus. It's that I'm working to be sure I cooperate with the Lord as He changes me to look like Jesus. It's exciting to be part of that process!

I don't intend to ever run a marathon. For those who love running, I know the pain of their physical training is worth it. But I do look forward to a prize of great gain. I look forward to becoming increasingly like Jesus. That is worth any sacrifice, any pain, any discipline. *"Let us run with endurance the race that lies before us keeping our eyes on Jesus, the author and perfecter of our faith"* (Hebrews 12:1-2, CSB).

After 35 years of full-time professional ministry, **Pat Conner** is loving life as a church consultant and ministry coach. She enjoys speaking and writing, but most of all loves being a wife, mother, and Nana to 5 boys, 3 girls, a number of grand-dogs, hundreds of grand-rabbits, and several prize-winning grand-goats.

chapter 4

FOR THE LOVE OF READING

You are stronger when you read.

BY LIZ-ANN AGUILLERA

THE JOURNEY THROUGH the halls of the bookstore, the haven of many a book lover, brings a mixture of ambivalent emotions of peace and excitement. The aroma of the paper, the anticipation of the latest arrivals, and the joy of sitting and thumbing through a book in the reading corner are all part of the experience. As a child my greatest pastime was reading. It brought solace during challenging times as I was whisked away into another world where I won battles, visited new countries, and solved crimes. I envisioned myself as the heroine of my stories, reading through so many books that I traded with other friends in order to engage in more adventures each week.

One day I was introduced to the greatest Book ever written, the B-I-B-L-E, which was definitely the book for me. My passion for reading was further fueled by accounts of great exploits and nuggets of wisdom in the hallowed pages, which sowed the seed of love for the Creator of all things. The Bible was not a dead book to me, but it was alive. I felt myself change daily as I read its pages.

"For the word of God is living and powerful, and sharper than any two-edged sword, piercing even to the division of soul and spirit, and of joints and marrow, and is a discerner of the thoughts and intents of the heart" (Hebrews 4:12, NKJV).

The Word is truly powerful. In Psalm 119:11 the reader is encouraged to hide or store it in their heart as a deterrent for sin. In the time that the Psalms were written, the Torah was read in the synagogue. Those who heard it had to memorize it, for there was no copy to refer to upon returning home, thereby, storing the Word of God in their heart. It was not until the invention of the printing press in the mid-15th century that the written Word was no longer limited to the privileged or ruling class but was also available to the masses. In modern times, it's a blessing to have access to digital books and audio books, a vast treasure trove of information.

FOR THE LOVE OF READING GOD'S WORD

Reading offers so much more than mere information or entertainment for the child of God. *"All Scripture is given by inspiration of God, and is profitable for doctrine, for reproof, for correction, for instruction in righteousness"* (2 Timothy 3:16, NKJV).

The Word provides doctrine, teaching, and learning. It's explicit on what the children of God believe. It teaches you, even as you read about the ultimate teacher, Jesus. The perfect template for teaching is provided by the Lord, who used stories and object lessons. Jesus used practical examples to explain abstract concepts and make them concrete. These explanations are timeless, relevant in current times and just as powerful. You can learn a lot about teaching by examining the strategies used by the Master.

Correction is often a hard pill to swallow. It is painful to correct a physical ailment. Mental ailments that take the form of poor attitudes and toxic mindsets are similarly challenging to change. Correction develops your character. The sharp characteristic of the Word of God is able to shine a light on the hidden and visible areas of your life that need to come into the perfection of Christ. As a teacher you are often the one giving correction to others. You also need to allow the spotlight to shine within so that you may first be corrected to be qualified to correct others. The beautiful thing about this situation is that God corrects you in love, and corrects you because He loves you. This is a pattern that everyone can abide by.

New appliances and gadgets come with an instruction manual, and they have earthly creators. Your heavenly Creator has provided you with one as well. It is profitable, helpful, and advantageous to read it. It gives you an advantage in life. You have inside knowledge on how and why you were designed as seen in Genesis 1:26-28 and 31. Man was fashioned, as a reflection of God, with similar attributes and given the mandate to be a fulfilled empowered leader in the earth that would produce more versions of Him. What an amazing purpose!

Many in this life live disenfranchised because they have not read the Word of God to know why they're here. They live aimlessly abusing the body they have been given. When you don't read the instruction manual about the equipment, you use it incorrectly and abuse it. Thank God for the Word, your manual, which is truly profitable for you. The Greek word for instruction in 2 Timothy 3:16 expounds on "the whole training and education of children (which relates to the cultivation of mind and morals, and employs for this purpose now commands and admonitions, now reproof and punishment)." (Strong's

Concordance) The Word is truly amazing, providing all that you need to teach your young charges about righteousness!

FOR THE LOVE OF DIVERSIFIED READING

The creative pull within me has developed a taste for a variety of reading topics. Learning new things causes new neuron connections in your brain, making it stronger, more agile, and adaptable to change. You are in the creative business, forever researching new methods of presenting the Gospel to an eager generation. A diversified reading plan will help you be better equipped in fulfilling this mandate.

Knowledge arbitrage involves using the knowledge and theories of one field and applying it to another field or industry. It can be viewed as a form of cross-pollination, sharing ideas that were developed in one system to benefit another. This knowledge can be garnered by reading genres including fiction, business, art, psychology, biography, science, and personal growth.

Fiction stimulates the imagination. Imagination is the playground of children. Storytelling is a foundational tool in children's ministry; a good story can make the Bible come to life to these young sponges. Reading fiction helps in structuring the parts of a good story and the use of descriptive words and phrases to paint a vivid image. I personally enjoy reading books written for children and books written by children so that I am able to use the patterns in my personal storytelling. This helps me in writing curriculum, as well as in viewing the material prepared from the perspective of a child to ensure that it is presented with relevance.

Business, and by extension management, are principles that help systems run effectively and efficiently. My personal profession is in the field of business, marketing to be exact. I've seen how business and management principles have been beneficial to children's ministry. You're responsible for managing resources and people. Reading books about business can help you plan and organize projects and programs in a way that is strategic. The importance of having objectives that are specific, measurable, attainable, realistic, and time bound, come from exposing yourself to these principles. Leadership philosophies such as transformational leadership, the use of action plans, and the importance of sustainability have helped me personally to implement systems in ministry that have allowed us to increase our reach immensely.

Art is a medium that can transcend language barriers. Colors can affect a person's mood, and the right decor in an environment can lead to the success or failure of a venture. My first degree is in graphic design, and being a visual learner myself, I have seen how the right or wrong use of art can be supportive or a distraction. I enjoy reading art history books, magazines, and blogs that focus on home, office, and stage design. These have inspired themes for lessons and innovative ways to make the teaching space appealing for learning.

Psychology is important for you to grasp, because you work with people, the majority of which are volunteers who need to be motivated. There are different theories or schools of thought on motivation, some of which include the Two Factor Theory of Motivation by Frederick Herzberg and Maslow's Hierarchy of Needs. My favorite motivational theory is the Three Needs Theory by psychologist David McClelland. This theory suggests that people are motivated by three major needs; the need for achievement, power, and affiliation. Some persons are encouraged to be a part of a group just to have a group that they belong to. That's affiliation. This is why it's important to have time to bond with ministry workers and volunteers to provide that sense of fellowship and camaraderie. Other persons are motivated by achievement, knowing that they have been able to be a part of a group that is accomplishing things that matter and make a difference. Then lastly, some persons are motivated by power, the ability to be in a leadership role and have input in decision making. This theory can be used to analyze the persons who are part of a team and ensure that they feel fulfilled in the role they play.

Eleanor Roosevelt once said "Learn from the mistakes of others. You can't live long enough to make them all yourself." This statement is apt to introduce the reading genre of biographies. Biographies are the accounts of lives of persons just like you, who chose to step out of the box and do extraordinary things. Their life stories often show their failures and their successes, their inner thoughts, moments of fear, and decisions to be courageous. Seeing examples of persons who chose the "road less travelled" inveigle hope, courage, and determination to the reader.

Science is a beautiful subject, when you see how it applies to practical living. Science is all around you, and many times it confirms accounts in the Bible. It is explorative and can stir up the passion for using investigation, experimentation, and attempting new ways of doing things. Science experiments can be used as object lessons to portray principles in the Word of God.

Personal growth is my all-time favorite reading category. A group can only grow as far as its leader grows. Personal growth books can cover areas such as time management, emotional intelligence, anger management, discipline, goal setting, and so on. As you work on yourself, your ways of thinking, and by extension, the way that you lead and execute your duties improve. There is no separation between you the children's ministry leader and you the individual. You are one and the same, and you have to lead yourself before you can lead others. Your stewardship of those you have been blessed to influence is predicated on your willingness to widen your capacity.

FOR THE LOVE OF READING, SHARE!

If you truly love someone, you want to share with him or her. And if you love something, you want to tell everyone about it. It's time to share the love of reading! There are different strategies that you can implement in order to share your love of reading with those around you.

These include:

1. Start a book club. Encourage the reading of books with the children and adults around you by initiating a book club. Engage in discussions and share what was enjoyable or impactful about the material.

2. Start a writing club. Avid readers often become avid writers. You always need more material to read; there are never enough books. Any true book-aholic would agree with me.

3. Sponsor a child in your community, church, or as a missions project with a Bible. I remember the impact that having a Bible had for me as a child. In many countries children still have limited access to education, and many have never seen, much less owned, a Bible. This would be planting a seed that will flourish in a child's heart and transform their entire outlook on life.

I end with this fitting quote, "The more that you read, the more things you will know. The more that you learn, the more places you'll go." (*I Can Read With My Eyes Shut!,* Dr. Seuss)

Liz-Ann Aguillera is a creative soul with a penchant for creative storytelling. At any moment she can be found singing a tune, giggling uncontrollably, or a combination of both.

chapter 5

WHEN REST ISN'T RESTFUL

*You are stronger when you
recalibrate to avoid burnout.*

BY CALEB HIGGINBOTHAM

I REMEMBER THE SENSE of excitement getting off the plane for the first time. It was enough to keep me energized seemingly forever. I was wrong. I was a new missionary, beginning my career in ministry by serving at a children's home in Mexico City (Niños de Mexico). Being there was incredible. Eager to work, I began passionately believing I could do everything. And I did everything. I helped raise 15 kids, translated letters, wrote biographies, was in charge of social media, and oversaw worship and youth at a local church. I lived life at an absurd pace, never taking time for myself. For about six months I lived this way. Then it hit me. Burnout.

Every leader risks experiencing burnout at some point; it seems inevitable. There are some things, though, that you can do to help avoid it. There are certain exercises and steps you can take every day to prevent burnout. One of the most important steps is taking time to recalibrate. When you regularly take time to retreat and recalibrate you become a stronger ministry leader, a stronger Christian, and a stronger person.

There are several extremely important lessons to learn to avoid burnout. First, not all rest is created equal, and not all rest replenishes. Physical rest doesn't guarantee spiritual health. You need physical rest, but you must never neglect your need to be active and engaged in something for replenishment. Like a computer, you must regularly take time to recalibrate. There are four means by which you can recalibrate: creativity, hobbies, taking care of your body, and spending time with others.

CREATIVITY

In Genesis 1 watch as God creates the world. Be amazed as He, *"hovers over the face of the waters"* (Genesis 1:2, ESV) and decides to create the world and humanity—His prized creation. It's the creation account where you see a picture of what God intends for life to be. Notice throughout the first two chapters of Genesis, God is creating. In Genesis 1:26 you learn that God created humanity in His image—His likeness. There's a magnitude of important theological impacts from this, but let's focus on the implication of humanity being created with an innate desire to be creative, like God is. Psychology supports the idea of humans longing to create.

Psychologists have found that the desire to do more and to create in new, innovative ways will never be satisfied; however, by seeking new ways to create you experience true feelings of fulfillment. Because God has hardwired humanity to be creative, you desire to create. Humans are the only species on the planet that uses creativity as a means to express and understand their emotions, and too often they fail to create because they believe the lie that not everyone has potential to be creative. Too many believe art is only for a minority. When you quit living the way God designed humanity to live, for whatever reason, your spiritual walk becomes unbalanced and you race toward burnout. Humans are not animals; you are made in God's very image and have a deep need to live the way He intended for you to live. By using the creativity that He has given, you live according to the intention He has for His creation. (I want to stress that while being creative is an important part of your job as a children's ministry leader, it is essential you be creative outside of work. You must create simply for the joy of it!)

Often, when an individual thinks of being creative, they think of comedians, musicians, actors, and performers; however, creativity takes on many forms. Unfortunately, there are too many men who believe that creativity is for women or it's not manly. Simply put, there is no truth to this idea. There are a variety of ways to be creative: playing guitar and learning to see the world in ways that make people laugh are two awesome ways.

Imagine a world without creativity. Imagine if you never learned to think differently. How sad would the world be if pool noodles were only used as pool noodles and never electric fences (something that the kids in my farm community do quite often)? Being creative will help you solve problems, learn to interact with children, make adults laugh, see joy in your everyday life, and even learn to see the positive in bad situations. God wired humans to be creative because without creativity you never improve, never experience what it truly means to bear His image, and never know how to have fun. Creativity comes in many forms: woodworking, music, cooking, poetry, painting, sewing, stand-up comedy, playing, even stories!

If you don't create you run the risk of never processing the world around you, and if you don't do that, then you can never make an impact on it. If you don't first accept the reality of a situation, then you will forever be inept to invoke any meaningful change. Creativity allows you to both accept the reality of every situation, and see solutions in ways only God can provide.

HOBBIES

Winston Churchill once said, "To be really happy and really safe, one ought to have at least two or three hobbies, and they must all be real." One of the key differences between good rest and wasted rest is how you spend your time. Too often people try to escape their problems by watching television, video games, or in any other way they can shut their brains off; however, you need to be investing in hobbies. Find something to love, something you can learn about passionately and spend hours doing.

Hobbies will lift your mood, they'll allow you to relax, and they help you realize how much you're capable of. When you start a new hobby, you're provided the opportunity to watch your progress, and be encouraged by your improvement, all while having fun. After all, that's what hobbies are for—fun and play. God tremendously blessed you by giving you play and joy as a means of worshipping Him.

If you don't already have a hobby, find one! If you do have one, spend time doing it! Hobbies are means by which you can experience joy, especially during hard times or burnout. Hobbies are anything you enjoy that you don't get paid for. Here's a list of some you can start: parkour, knife throwing, coffee, fishing, collecting coins, gardening, magic tricks, puzzles, and comedy.

TAKING CARE OF YOUR BODY

If you ever ask a runner why they run you may be surprised by their answer. Certainly they run for health, but often it has little to do with their physical health. Often, they simply enjoy running as a means of relaxation, stress relief, and a time to pray and meditate. If you don't participate in regular exercise then you're setting yourself up to experience burnout. Daily exercise is crucial to recalibrating and not only making it through burnout, but emerging stronger from it.

In the creation account, Adam worked, physically labored, before the fall ever occurred. God designed Adam, and all of humanity, for work and being physically active (Genesis 2:15). In 1 Timothy 4:7-8 Paul says, *"Have nothing to do with irreverent, silly myths. Rather train yourself for godliness; for while bodily training is of some value, godliness is of value in every way, as it holds promise for the present life and also for the life to come"* (1 Timothy 4:7-8, ESV). While this verse is, admittedly, pushing toward spiritual exercise, it recognizes that training to be godly involves your physical health and its impact on your spiritual well-being. God has intertwined your spiritual and physical life in such a way that when one is in distress the other greatly suffers.

The emotional and physical benefits of taking care of your body are overwhelming! Regular aerobic exercise helps fight depression, improves your mood and quality of sleep, and reduces your stress and anxiety levels. Aerobic exercise has even been found to help improve verbal memory and learning abilities and thus helps fight against dementia. Some research suggests that with as little as five minutes of daily aerobic exercise, you can begin to experience these benefits. It is, in part, because of this that caring for your body is an essential part of recalibrating yourself.

God designed you to be physically active. This means your physical reality directly impacts your spiritual reality. If you feel like you've hit a plateau in your spiritual walk, or that you need to recalibrate, then get out and exercise. Run, walk, play soccer or basketball, ride a bike, or swim. God designed you to live a physically active life, and to not live this way keeps you outside of God's intention for your body, thus feeling a perpetual sense of unease.

Taking care of your body is perhaps the single biggest factor of being able to recalibrate and avoid burnout. This isn't achieved by exercise alone. It's essential you eat healthily. Proverbs 23:20 says, *"Be not among drunkards or among gluttonous eaters of meat"* (Proverbs 23:20, ESV). To use such strong wording as, *"be not among,"* it must be incredibly important to God that you don't overeat. Everyone struggles with overeating or eating poorly; however, when you want to lose weight you can't set goals like "lose five pounds and have all the biscuits and gravy you want." This doesn't help. God has designed your body to eat a certain way, and to ignore that is risky. Overeating makes you feel sick, fat, contributes to depression, and lowers your self-esteem. But eating properly, while a difficult choice to make, results in better self-esteem, improved mood, more energy, and better health! Your body has been intricately created by God as His temple, and deserves to be treated as such. You must learn to eat healthily as it will revitalize you and allow you to have more energy and feel better. It is, after all, God's plan.

SPENDING TIME WITH OTHERS

The only part of creation God declared "not good" was man being alone. Later in the New Testament, when Jesus sent out His disciples, He sent them in groups of two. Every time Paul went on a missionary journey he had others accompany Him. You are created to be in community. You can best see the importance of community by observing God Himself. God is triune. He is three persons in one God. Community is in His very nature. The Father, Son, and Spirit have been in perfect communion with one another before time existed. Therefore, being made in God's image means you need, and even crave, community. You need friends.

Psychologists believe one of the most important keys to human happiness is friends. They've found all humanity craves three essential things in life: safety, a sense of belonging, and knowing that you matter. Friends provide a sense of all three essential emotions. Psychologists aren't alone in recognizing the profound impact of friendship on our lives; the Bible teaches this as well. Proverbs 27:9-10 says, *"Oil and perfume make the heart glad, and the sweetness of a friend comes from his earnest counsel. Do not forsake your friend and your father's friend, and do not go to your brother's house in the day of you˙ calamity. Better is a neighbor who is near than a brother who is far away"* (Proverbs 27:9-10, ESV).

Friends have the unique ability to speak truth into your life that you would never allow others to even think. Whether you realize it or not, you give your friends a position of power in your life to sharply rebuke you when needed, and lift you up during a time of need. They provide a place where you can safely be yourself and a group to which you belong where there is no judgement.

Friends play a key role in defining an individual's priorities and mission in life, but they also deeply impact one's health. Researchers have found that older people with close friends are less likely to develop chronic diseases than those without close friends. Similarly, young people with close friends are less likely to suffer from depression. None of this should be surprising because the Bible teaches the importance of friendship by saying in Romans 12:15, *"Rejoice with those who rejoice; weep with those who weep"* (ESV). It is this precise role of friendship that is intended to encourage during periods of turmoil and burnout. There is one other way friends are a treasure, and unfortunately, too often, it's overlooked.

Everyone longs to matter and friends provide you that very opportunity. No one wants to be a burden to their friends, but the truth is, you are. It's good to burden your friends. It's why you have them, and they want you to burden them; however, the truest blessing of friendship is providing counsel to your friends. You're awarded the privilege of mattering by being there for them. When you care for your friends and listen to them in their time of need, you're impacting their lives in a very real way. It's exactly this give-and-take in a friendship that will provide you with a sense of mattering. Friends help you to recalibrate by pointing you to the reality of your situation and the truth of God.

Finally, know that real rest doesn't require a total retreat away from people. Rather, by taking time every day to recalibrate you can avoid burnout completely. Recharge by committing an hour every day to turn off your phone and television. (I do this at dinner time with my family.) Dedicate one day every week, and take at least one week every year to completely unplug from technology. Spend the time, instead, talking with one another and investing in one of the many things you can do to recalibrate. Spend time in a hobby, creating music as a family, cooking together, telling stories, making up stories, inventing silly games, or being outside together. This is what God had in mind when He created the Sabbath. Families were meant to spend time together, and you were created with a need to rest. In Genesis, God rested on the seventh day after creating the world. He ceased His creating and took time to simply enjoy it. God saw the value in rest and did it, yet too many children's leaders believe they're too busy or important to take a full day off and rest.

The next time you need rest, make sure you have a truly restful day. Remember, not all rest is restful. Spend time in a new hobby, exercising, being with friends, or creating. The beautiful thing about each of these is they don't have to be done separately from one another. Make music with friends on your day off. Find an indoor soccer league. Make new friends. You are stronger when you take time to rest.

Caleb Higginbotham is a children's minister in Fairfield, IL. He loves his wife, son, tacos, and music. His favorite thing to do is be outside making his friends laugh and creating up silly games!

chapter 6

LOVE IN THE MIDST OF LOGISTICS

*You are stronger when you
overcome not being able to be in corporate worship.*

BY KAT ALVARADO

L OGISTICS. WEEK AFTER WEEK my job consists of a plethora of logistics. A Sunday morning in children's ministry is as beautifully complicated as any intricate machine. There are the days every volunteer shows up, on time, and they have every item they need to make the morning run smoothly as they teach the goodness of Jesus to the sweetest faces. On those days every child who comes through our doors is well rested and well fed. Those children are excited to see their teacher, and they aren't feeling shy, nervous, or rambunctious. On those days, I head into the sanctuary with a heart ready to worship Jesus with my church body and ready to hear the Spirit speak to me through the Word of the Lord. I sit with my phone next to me completely silent, and I am uplifted, challenged, and ready to go out and serve Jesus with every ounce of my being. Those days are just so good. They are like a sweet, perfectly ripe strawberry—that kind that leaves juice dripping down your chin as you eat it on a sweltering summer day; they are glorious. But those days are not my normal.

Logistics are my normal. How do I rearrange classrooms to fit the kids I have and the volunteers I don't? How do I help the new foster child adjust when he/she can't sit still for more than 30 seconds? What last minute craft can I help a teacher with when they left everything they prepped at home? What resource do I have for the family who just lost someone dear to them? Where is the original label for the classroom snack for a new allergy mom who just needs to know that her child will be safe without her in the room? What videos do I have to replace the video the teacher wanted that won't play correctly? Logistics, logistics, logistics.

Being a children's ministry director means being able to put out a thousand little fires each week so that the people around you can serve Jesus, spend time at Jesus' feet, and have their souls restored.

I bet the Martha we meet in Luke 10 would have been a great children's ministry director. I bet she would have had the VBS snack for 500 kids down to an exact science. She would have had the schedule mapped out and executed with precision. She would have been amazing. People would have praised her for her hard work and God-given talents of management and organization. The people who served under Martha would have been well cared for spiritually and physically.

If you're honest, you see a bit of yourself in Martha. You are a doer. You work hard for the benefit of others, and you have the best motivation. You want to please Jesus. You want people to respond to Jesus. You want others to know the hope you have. You want the children in your care to be linked in a loving relationship with the God who created them. You want good things! And if that means that you teach two services on Sundays, teach another on Wednesday night, all while prepping for VBS, then, by golly, that's exactly what you're going to do! But, if you're like me, and you feel convicted, not encouraged, when you read the story of Martha, you're in good company, my friend.

You see, I'm in the position of children's ministry director because God has called me to it and designed me for it. And when I am at my best, I am doing what He made me to do. But I can often take what He made for good and turn it into something, well, less than. That's the story of mankind though, isn't it?

Let's look at Martha's story.

"Now it happened as they went that He entered a certain village; and a certain woman named Martha welcomed Him into her house. And she had a sister called Mary, who sat at Jesus' feet and heard His word. But Martha was distracted with much serving, and she approached Him and said, 'Lord, do you not care that my sister has left me to serve alone? Therefore, tell her to help me.' And Jesus answered and said to her, 'Martha, Martha, you are worried and troubled about many things. But one thing is needed, and Mary has chosen that good part, which will not be taken away from her'" (Luke 10:38-42, NKJV).

I hear my voice in Martha's voice. I hear her with my soul, not just my ears. She's asking for help, because she's running the show. She has planned out and is executing all the logistics. She is overwhelmed and feeling like she's carrying the weight of the world on her shoulders. She, the master of logistics, is drowning in them. And she cries out to Jesus. But even in her crying out she is telling Jesus, the Maker and Sustainer of everything, how He can efficiently and effectively solve her problems. (That Martha, she really is just so helpful.)

When I start reading this story, I feel what Martha is saying, but I also feel *for* her. I mean, I know what it's like when a task I delegated gets dropped and now I must do it, myself, last minute. Or the Sunday mornings when my phone blows up with text after text of teachers dropping like flies. I start to cry out, "Jesus, tell them to help me! Don't you see me doing everything? Convict them, Holy Spirit! I need You to get them to help me!" But it is never long before I hear my name in Jesus' gentle rebuke. "Kat, Kat you are worried and troubled about many things (logistics!). But one thing is needed (I know, send me more help Jesus!), and Mary has chosen that good part, which will not be taken from her. (But Jesus, how can I choose the better part? *Someone* needs to serve in children's ministry. *Someone* needs to plan VBS. *Someone* needs to snuggle that kiddo who just needs a hug today. *I wish I could* be in the service. Wouldn't that be nice... to just show up to church and sit down and worship! If you do not hear a snarky tone in those words, go back and read it dripping in snark, because that's how it plays in my head.

On my bad days—on my days when I want to feel like a victim and forget that I am thankful for my call into ministry, when I want to wallow in self pity and forget about all my sins that were paid for on the cross, when I want to feel like God needs to pat me on the back for all the good work I have done for Him. I am close to missing the truth in that exchange between Jesus and Martha from Luke 10. Jesus didn't chastise her for serving. The service was an expectation. It was her home; she should have served them. She should have prepared food and made room. And she did. But then, she saw something on Pinterest and needed to add to what she had already done. (That's not accurate, but I feel like Martha would have been all about Pinterest if it had existed then. Or if computers did. Or electricity. Whatever, I think you get my point.) She didn't know when to stop and sit. She forgot she was a human being, and instead tried to be a human-doing. She had logistics-itis. And I do, too.

God absolutely called me to ministry. And my ministry requires a great deal of logistics. When teachers call in sick, or something needs to be addressed now, the buck stops with me. So how on earth do I learn to sit and be in Jesus' presence and purposefully worship and praise Him when my job keeps me out of a church service sometimes months at a time? Well, luckily for me, the same Jesus who loved and created Martha the way she was, loves and created me the way I am. He knows that I need to be reminded of His presence and my need for it, often and loudly.

Last year our morning VBS had just ended for the day, and, man, had it been a day of craziness. It had been the kind of day where my feet screamed, "Put me up!"... the kind of day where my cup of coffee migrated all over the entire church campus, and yet went completely untouched the whole day. After the last child left, and the only thing left to do was check that everything was off in the sanctuary, Jesus gently called me to worship. As I walked in, in a complete self-focused pity party my-feet-ache kind of flurry, I looked up and saw the backlight to the large cross on the wall was still on. Begrudgingly, I went into the quiet, cool, mostly dark room to (insert sigh) shut it off. That was when I felt the presence of my God wash over me. It was all at once, heavy and thick yet light and airy. It was the kind of feeling I assume Jacob felt in Genesis 28 as he had the dream of angels ascending and descending the staircase from heaven to earth, with God standing at the top. I sat in a chair in front of the cross; I wept, I smiled, and I sang. I hadn't realized how thirsty I was for His presence until I felt it, and I almost missed it. I was so worried and troubled about many things, all good things, all important things, that I almost missed the *most* important thing. I almost missed my Bethel moment. The Lord was there, and I was so busy serving that I almost missed Him!

The logistics of my job can be fierce, but I am stronger when I find moments with God, even if they aren't afforded to me on a Sunday morning.

The trap of the self-righteous pity-party is a well-hidden trap. It lies between a busy Sunday and busy week. It hides beneath deadlines and a full inbox. It waits patiently like a skilled hunter for the days I am "too busy" to spend time at the Lord's feet. And the trap sucks the life-giving hope and joy of Jesus from me like a dry sponge soaks up water. Satan is a lying liar who lies. And he likes to tell me that I am too important, that my tasks are too important, to wait. He inflates my ego with my self-importance and yet at the same time sucks the life from me. Being inflated and deflated at the same time seems impossible. Yet, as a Martha I am quite good at it. When I think I am too important to stop and sit at Jesus' feet I am lying to myself, and even worse, sinning against my God. When I think the world will stop spinning if I stop and worship, then I am saying God can't do it without me. And I am saying He can't sustain me, or that "my" ministry (as if it were ever actually run, sustained, or caused to grow by my own power anyway), would suffer without my constant hyper-vigilance.

Instead, what I need to learn, and am just beginning to grasp fully, is that my service to others must always come second to the most important thing ever—my relationship with Jesus. And while the members of my church may be blessed with a scheduled time slot for worship every Sunday from 9:30-10:45, I often am not. So being that I am blessed to be called to ministry, I must find more moments like my Bethel moment after VBS. I sneak these moments in during the week when I do "office work." Sometimes I head down to the sanctuary and sit in the cool, dark, quiet room. I pray, I sing worship songs to my Jesus, I hear Him. And It. Is. So. Good.

My soul also finds great refreshment and rest by being part of a mid-week Bible study. I attend my local Community Bible Study where nothing depends on my handling logistics. Though I struggle each week with attending because part of me says, "I need more me time!" I have never once regretted going. The truth is that I don't need more "me time"; I need more scheduled time to spend at Jesus' feet each week. I get to show up. Just show up. And I get to discuss God's Word with a group of ladies who love Jesus. I get to sing in worship with a body of believers, and I get to listen to the lecture and hear God's still small voice speak to my heart in conviction, connection, and comfort. My scheduled time at Jesus' feet isn't consistently on Sundays, but it is consistently on Thursdays from 10:00-11:45. And It. Is. So. Good.

Being blessed with the chance to teach children about Jesus, I also get to model worship for them. The days when I lead them in worship, I am not just singing empty words, but communing with the Author and Sustainer of my faith. The Lord is there in every classroom, the way He is in the sanctuary, the way He is in my car, and everywhere else for that matter. So, if I am aiming my heart at His, then I am worshiping. And do you know what I love about worshiping with kids? They aren't worried about how their voice sounds, and they aren't worried about how others are looking at them. They sing like they are singing for an audience of one—Jesus. I learn a lot about letting go of myself when I worship with children.

God is working on me. Each day He is painting another scene across the canvas of my life, and right now that scene includes a great deal of work and logistics, for the benefit of others. And even though the lying liar who lies tries to convince me to be bitter about it, I wouldn't change this season for the world. I am learning to be a Marthy... you know, a cross between Martha and Mary. I am learning to serve and also be present. I am learning to lead and to worship. I am learning to find my strength in the sustenance of my Jesus. And It. Is. So. Good.

Five years ago, **Kat Valarado** was a stay-at-home mom with 2 kids in public school and a toddler at home, completely unaware of the roller coaster God had planned for her. Now she is a children's ministry director and homeschool mom who survives on the love of Jesus and a bit of coffee.

chapter 7

A SPIRITUAL KICK

*You are stronger when you
identify your sources of inspiration.*

BY RACHAEL JOHNSON

EVERYONE HAS A DESIRE to be strong. You desire to be stronger, slightly better today than you were yesterday. In most cases, you want instant gratification—a quick fix. When a new diet or work-out system comes around that looks easy and promises immediate results, people are interested. How about a quicker, easier way to cook? You want it to look good, taste good, but you really don't want to work for it. The same could be said even for your spiritual life. If you think God has not responded to your "issue" or answered quick enough, you start trying to fix it yourself or look for someone or something to fix it for you. Admit it, if someone told you they had a quick, measurable way to grow your ministry and its impact, your ears would perk up. What person in children's ministry isn't constantly looking for a new idea or approach to make following God easier for children and families? The truth is, there are no spiritual shortcuts. Sometimes, you just need a "spiritual kick." Instead of looking at the immediate, let's look at the big picture. What is it that causes children's ministers to get up daily, even when your mind is fatigued and your physical body is exhausted? You're inspired by the big picture ... the end goal ... your why. Therefore, you are stronger when you identify and utilize your sources of inspiration.

IDENTIFYING IN-GOD-SPIRATION

The word *inspire* comes from the Latin meaning, "to breathe life into." So, what inspires you, makes you feel alive? Many people refer to nature, being outdoors, taking walks, listening to music, creating or observing art, reading scripture, or hearing testimonies of others succeeding. These are great references of inspiration. What do all of these things have in common? The Source! God Himself is the root, the center, breathing life into all that brings inspiration. *"Looking unto Jesus the author and perfecter of our faith"* (Hebrews 12:2, ASV). He is the creator.

> *"The Lord merely spoke, and the heavens were created. He breathed the word, and all the stars were born. He assigned the sea its boundaries and locked the oceans in vast reservoirs. Let the whole world fear the Lord and let everyone stand in awe of him. For when he spoke, the world began"* (Psalm 33:6-9, NLT).

If that doesn't inspire you, I don't know what will! There is no denying that when you witness or are reminded of His beauty in this world and in His people, it's as if someone (the Holy Spirit) is breathing "life into you."

Inspiration awakens you to new possibilities and even transforms the way you perceive your own capabilities. It's not until you become actively inspired, creating things, applying ideas, and even making mistakes that you propel forward. Sometimes it may even feel like a spiritual kick. It gives you momentum to go further or dig deeper. "The inspiration is not the receiving of information. The inspiration is applying what you've received." (Derek Sivers) For example, when you hear from the Holy Spirit, it's amazing, but it's not until you apply, or do as He has instructed that you are truly inspired beyond your own limitations—much like an awakening to something better, transcending your own ideas or visions. It's during those times of intimacy with Him that you can be reminded of your purpose as well as the treasures, trials, and victories you have walked through.

TREASURES AND TRIALS

Have you ever thought of failures or trials as a source of inspiration? For example, yesterday when three of the volunteers didn't show up for service and the technology you needed for your lesson decided the "server could not be found", you had a minor meltdown. Today, however, you're scheduling double the workers needed for the upcoming service and making good old flash cards for back up. Yesterday's trials motivated you— gave you a desire—to do better so you would have a more favorable, immediate result. Could you possibly find inspiration from those times when very few people showed up for an event you and your team worked so hard to put on, or you had that very unhappy parent to deal with? Maybe you didn't handle things gracefully with a co-worker or at the end of the day you were unable to cross absolutely nothing off your very long to-do list.

How do you find inspiration in those things? For one, you survived! Praise God, Hallelujah! Coming through the other side of a failure is worthy of celebration. I know personally, I try to recognize the bright side and give God glory for even what seems to be the smallest victory at the time. Those are treasures! Thank you, Jesus, the child who decided to paint his face in class today was not allergic to red dye. Or, praise God you had on dark undergarments when your pants ripped open after demon-strating how Goliath fell to the ground. Although I'm giving ex-amples of somewhat humorous trials, you know there are more substantial trials that appear as mountains in your path of min-istry—some bigger and more stressful than others.

On more than one occasion I have witnessed crisis. In the midst of the crisis I witnessed grace and upon overcoming the crisis I experienced revelation. You can attest to the goodness of God when you overcome and reflect on such trials in your life and in your ministry. *"Get up and stand to your feet, for I have appeared to you to reveal your destiny and to commission you as my assistant"* (Acts 26:16, TPT). When you face fail-ures, trials, or crisis, you experience and utilize the power of your purpose which gives you the energy and courage to keep moving forward.

YOUR "WHY"

Let's identify the purpose behind not quitting. There is a drive, a confidence in knowing your purpose, that motivates you to keep getting back up each time. When you know your "why"—why you continue to live the way you do, why you believe what you believe, why you're willing to fail—you will become stron-ger because you're inspired by the end goal.

Our society places great importance on what you do or what you acquire, which promotes a tendency to think of it as your purpose. Let's put this in kidmin terms. Your purpose should not be based off the number of kids in your ministry, the size of your budget, or the number of hours you put in weekly. All of those things could change drastically or even perish and you should still be living within your purpose.

Another misconception people have about their purpose is that it's based on their role or personal abilities. For example, what happens when you think that being a good children's minister or leader is your life's purpose, but you have children who fall into the traps of the world. They become very different than you had hoped. Or maybe you didn't witness the number of salvations you had expected. Are you a failure? This is when wounding self-judgment takes place. Your life purpose must be bigger than your role, larger than yourself or your agenda. It must be long lasting, enduring, yet flexible. It is the very thing that guides your life decisions, influences your behavior, shapes your goals, creates meaning, and provides a sense of direction. *"A person may have many ideas concerning God's plan for his life, but only the designs of his purpose will succeed in the end"* (Proverbs 19:21, TPT). A clear sense of purpose enables you to focus your efforts on what matters most, compelling you to take on challenges that stretch you as much as they inspire you. You push forward regardless of the odds or obstacles.

INSPIRATION IN VISION

A life inspired by purpose is a life defined by vision and meaning rather than roles and stuff. ("The Purpose-Inspired Life", Carl Golden) When you are inspired or awakened to something new, there are moments of clarity. You're able to see things you may not have seen before. They say inspiration happens to you, and that it is not willed. However, God gave you the power of choice. You can choose where you focus and who you focus on. Personally, I've found that when I focus on God and do His will, I am reminded of my purpose. Working with kids, you know that visuals are a necessity. Have you ever thought about putting your life purpose and vision in front of you to serve as a reminder, encouragement, and inspiration along your purposeful path? Not only will it become clear to you, but will be an amazing example to those in your life and in your circle of influence. You're probably thinking, what does that look like?

I'm referring to a vision board. Some entrepreneurs are encouraged to create vision boards of personal goals they want to achieve or work towards. Why not do this in regard to your life purpose? Create a clear picture of what shapes your life from concept to reality. It can be big or small. A picture, a poster board, or even a bulletin board, made of whatever you have or whatever you want. Knowing the audience reading this is filled with creative kidmin teams, I can only imagine the amazing finished products. (Maybe even hints of glitter!) This is something you can do with your children in your ministry as well. For years, I did this with my kindergartners in the public school system. They loved it! The sooner you realize your purpose, the better! Children are filled with the spirit of possibilities, more so than adults. Regardless of your past, you need to return to that childlike innocence when it comes to dreaming, speaking, and living out the possibilities of your life.

Let's start with your core values. What do you stand for and willing to give your life towards? Who are you and what can people count on you for? Remember, it's more about *who* you are, not *what* you do, and *how* you do it. This is when I open my Bible and start declaring who He says I am. Are you starting to get ideas? Feeling inspired? I think you will find that the process of creating a vision board is so inspiring, because it pushes you to physically put words and pictures on paper. You know what's in your "knower", but when you begin to see your purpose in front of you, it gives direction. *"Set your gaze on the path before you. With fixed purpose, looking straight ahead, ignore life's distractions. Watch where you're going! Stick to the path of truth, and the road will be safe and smooth before you"* (Proverbs 4:25-26, TPT).

LEAD STRONGER

As you can see there is not a quick fix, superhero power to make you instantly stronger as a leader in kidmin. There are, however, many voices, lots of volume, tons of experiences, and many amazing people within children's ministry who can inspire you. It's a choice to lead with a grateful, joyful heart—a path you have chosen to walk, a job that aligns with your life purpose. *"Care for the flock that God has entrusted to you. Watch over it willingly, not grudgingly—not for what you will get out of it, but because you are eager to serve God"* (1 Peter 5:1-4, NLT).

People watch what you do and listen to what you say, especially those you lead. You must lead authentically and intentionally by example, communicating with passion and purpose. When you know where your inspiration comes from and how to utilize it, the people you lead will also. As they see you finding strength through trials, they will strive to be stronger. As they see you walk out your life purpose, they will begin defining their own. As you lay out your vision, they will find clarity. When you become stronger and better today than you were yesterday, so will those around you.

Rachael Johnson loves to give and has an obvious love for children. She enjoys decorating and is slightly obsessed with things that match.

chapter 8

NO MORE LIES

You are stronger when I put fear in its place.

BY TARA BLANKINSHIP

IT WAS A SUNDAY night. I had been in the interview process for what felt like a lifetime, but that night was the worst night of all. I was 23 at the time, fresh out of college, and applying to be the children's director of a church with an older congregation... much older than me anyway. In fact, there was only one other couple in their 20s. It was a very traditional church and my age was a hot topic. At my last interview (of a 3-interview set) I was invited to an ice cream social in which anyone from the church was welcome to attend and ask me questions. I was then asked to leave so they could confer as a church. A phone call would come in the next hour or so to tell me what the church had decided.

I waited by the phone. I played the interview over and over in my head. "How do you plan to be a leader without any experience?" "Is this the job you want, or just something to keep you busy until you find the next big thing?" "What makes you qualified to do this job at only 23?" And the questions continued on a loop in my head.

As I continued to wait for the call, I got busy overthinking it. Maybe they're right. Maybe I have no right to be applying for this position. Maybe my inexperience is too much to allow my success in this well-established traditional church. Maybe I'm setting myself up for failure. Maybe this isn't really what God's calling me to. Maybe, just maybe, I should withdraw my application now. The "maybes" kept multiplying in my head.

While the fear of what people thought of me continued to creep in, my phone rang. It was the pastor. I got the job. Maybe they really did like me after all. Maybe.

TWO TYPES OF FEAR

There are two kinds of fears: healthy fears and unhealthy fears. A healthy fear is motivated by facts. For example: Fire is hot. Fire can burn. Letting my 2-year-old play near a candle causes me fear, because she could get hurt. This healthy fear leads me to put out the candle to prevent a potentially bad situation.

An unhealthy fear is something that's motivated by lies and unknowns—a fear that, at its core, aims to prevent a potentially good outcome. For instance, my story above. "Am I good enough? Is this really what God called me to?" An unhealthy fear is something that defies the logic that's already known. I had already felt called. I already knew that God is good even when I am not. I already knew the truth that this is where I was meant to be, but my fear brought that calling into question. Unhealthy fear is not based on common knowledge. None of us knows what the future holds. Fears based solely on "what ifs" and "maybes" are what I call an unhealthy fear. That is not from God. The enemy uses fear as a tactic to keep people from advancing His kingdom.

Unhealthy fear is just that—unhealthy. It's from the enemy. One thing that needs to be understood about the enemy is that he did not get to be the enemy by putting up a weak fight. Unhealthy fear goes against logic; it goes against the truth that God has already told you. It's not based on facts or common knowledge. Despite all of the facts, I can also state that unhealthy fear is convincing.

This fear, when it works its ways into your thoughts and simmers there, it has the power to become all consuming. Fear has the power to change your perception of what is true. It has the power to keep you from your call.

Let me put this more practically. The fear from the enemy has the power to lead you to procrastinate on plans that can make your ministry better. It has the power to convince you to make safe choices rather than taking the risks that you feel God may be calling your ministry to take. It has the power to make a leader give in to the opinions of others, or even what they think their opinions are, rather than making the hard calls—the potentially better calls. Fear has the power to make someone want to give up while they're ahead, or before they get further behind.

THE PREVENTATIVE FACTORS

In order to prevent fear from encroaching in life and in ministry, it is important to:

1. Keep your eye on the prize.
2. Understand the difference between healthy fear and unhealthy fear.
3. Set up safe guards through safe people.
4. Stay in the Word and in prayer.

KEEP YOUR EYE ON THE PRIZE

What is your calling? What is your goal? Where do you think God is leading you? What is your purpose? It's important to know the answers to these questions, because it's the answers to these questions that the enemy will be out to destroy. Once the prize can be identified, it becomes easier to be aware of the enemy's plot to interfere.

Understand the difference between healthy fear and unhealthy fear. The type of fear is not only determined by the subject matter, but also by the intensity in which it creates an impact. Know this: if fear hits a person on a deep emotional level, it is not healthy! Let me backtrack a bit to my example of my 2-year-old playing near a lit candle. If I see my daughter climbing up on the table to look at the candle, it is healthy for me to feel alarmed and take action. It is not healthy, however, for me to see my daughter eying the candle and to be so afraid of the danger and the "what ifs" that could happen if she touched it or knocked it over that it keeps me from doing what I need to do—protect her. It is possible to be so startled by something that a healthy fear turns unhealthy—when it goes from something to consider to something crippling. Fear should not keep you up at night. Fear should not be the basis of how decisions are made. Fear should not stand in the way of God's calling. That is not from God. Fear is a liar, friends. Know the truth, because knowing what is true will make it easier to better identify what is not.

SETTING UP SAFEGUARDS THROUGH SAFE PEOPLE

Knowing what the goal is and identifying fears early are both safeguards. But when left only to one's own self you can sometimes get so wrapped up by what scares you that you allow fear to break down those walls. The lines become blurry and the lies of the enemy start to feel like truths. I am a frequent offender in this regard. To avoid this, I have a trusted friend who is also in ministry and we get together weekly. We talk about what our goals are and share our fears. If I ever get into a spot where my fears feel all-consuming or I am too much "in my head", I trust her to repeat back to me the things I told her on my good days when my fears were not disrupting my decision making. If I am proactive in sharing with my trusted friend, she can act as a safeguard by reminding me of my truths on days when I am not at my best.

STAYING IN THE WORD AND IN PRAYER

This isn't a secret. Even as toddlers it is preached to "read your Bible, pray every day, pray every day, pray every day." (Side note: If you didn't sing that as you read it, you're missing out on a great song.) I did not save this point for last because it's least important, but rather because it is the absolute most important. If the goal is to put fear in its place, staying in the Word is not optional. When I graduated from high school my youth pastor gifted me a new Bible. When he handed it to me he said this: "Either this book will keep you from sin, or sin will keep you from this book. There is no other outcome." That has stuck with me ever since.

"The thief's purpose is to steal and kill and destroy. My purpose is to give them a rich and satisfying life" (John 10:10, NLT). If I am not remaining in constant communication with the One who gives life, then I'm making myself vulnerable to the one whose purpose is to steal, kill, and destroy. Fear is a slippery slope. In order to avoid the trap that is the lies of the enemy, it is essential to draw near to the One who gives truth.

HOW DO I PUT FEAR IN ITS PLACE ONCE I'M ALREADY KNEE DEEP?

The enemy does not like to see people working to advance the kingdom of the Lord. For those who have chosen to devote their lives to doing so, they have become big targets. Despite setting safeguards, there are likely going to be times when fear takes over. What then? The enemy's goal is to get God's people off course. Whatever the goal is, whatever the calling or the purpose, if it is something that will lead to the bettering of a ministry and the advancement of the Kingdom, the enemy will see it as a threat. I've spent a lot of years allowing fear to be my demise. Through those times I've learned a lot about setting safeguards to prevent myself from getting to that place, but I've also learned how to come out of it. These are my steps.

1. Fall back on your safeguards.
2. Don't make any decisions out of fear.
3. Keep moving forward.

FALL BACK ON YOUR SAFEGUARDS

Safeguards are wonderful because not only do they help as a preventative measure, but they're also there to help as a rescue measure when fear has found its way in. Be reminded of what the prize is. Identify the present fears. Call up that trusted friend and confront the fears audibly. Most importantly, lay it all at the feet of Jesus. Take it to prayer, get in the Word, be reminded of His truth.

DON'T LET FEAR MAKE THE DECISIONS

Take a deep breath! Sit back. Look at the big picture. Being a leader in ministry means sometimes needing to make the hard calls and the fear that comes with that can be crippling. Do not make a decision because fear demanded it. Make decisions with purpose and not out of compliance to what scares you or what feels most comfortable. God has been teaching me a big lesson over the past year and it is this: **It is better to glorify God through making people angry than to satisfy people by complying with the lies of the enemy.** In the end, it's your responsibility to follow the Lord. Rest in that. Really take that in. If your focus is set on the big picture and what God is calling you to do, the fears of what can go wrong will be diminished.

Are you afraid people will get angry? So what if they do, if you did what was right? Are you afraid it won't go perfectly, wonderfully right? It probably won't. But if you're following the leading of the Spirit, it will go as it should.

KEEP MOVING FORWARD

Fear has the power to hold you back. If a person is afraid of what they're going to do, it can become easier to just sit back and do nothing. Know what is right and push through the fear. Many times, the fear of the unknown is worse than knowing the truth and getting it over with.

Know that God will not call you to do something just to leave you stranded. He will be there with you. Rest in Him and know that whatever the short term may hold, He has a bigger purpose for what you are doing right now.

It's a Sunday evening. I'm in my quiet time thanking God for the journey He has brought me through in my time in children's ministry. I would not be here if I had given in to the fear I had that day of my last interview. I may not even be here if I had accepted the job, but allowed those "maybes" to continue playing through my mind. I may not be here if I had let the fears of making people angry keep me from following God's will. God has been taking me on a journey of learning to stop fear in its tracks. Through that journey, He has made me stronger.

Tara Blankinship has a degree in social work, but was called into children's ministry fresh out of college and is currently serving as the Children's Ministry Director at Gospel Center Missionary Church in South Bend, IN. She has 2 biological children as well as a third child through foster care.

chapter 9

"NO" IS A 3-LETTER WORD

You are stronger when you're able to say no.

BY AANNA SMALLEY

WHY IS "NO" one of the hardest words for those in ministry to say? Pastors are servants and givers and lovers, self-less, compassionate and willing to do whatever it takes. No wonder it can be hard to say *no*. A few years ago I read the book *Present Over Perfect* by Shauna Niequist and the value of my *yeses* and *nos* became more evident to me than ever. She said, "Every time you say yes to one thing, you say no to everything else. You can't have yes without no. Another way to say it: If you're not careful with your yeses, you start to say no to some very important things without even realizing it." This thought was totally new to me. It seems strange for me to write that it never crossed my mind that saying yes to so many things also meant I was saying no to lots of other things. It just makes sense. Maybe some of you are in the same space I was when I first read that.

I really do believe that I'm stronger when I'm able to say no to some things.

I want to be upfront with you and share that this is still very much a work in progress for me. Just last week I sat in a meeting with my kidmin team, explaining a new form that we asked staff to fill out along with their leave requests. I mentioned that the new form wasn't complete yet, but I'd be getting to it as soon as I was able. One of the kidmin pastors on my team boldly called me out and said, "Aanna, you have too much on your plate right now and you don't need to be the one doing that. You told us that we need to watch what we give our yeses to." So, I'm writing this with a side of humble pie for snack. I promise you that I know this struggle all too well.

Let's chat about this "no" business! Some of you may be really self-aware right out of the gate that you are king or queen of *yes*! You may even pride yourself on that a little. So often this is a great trait to have. You may very well be the one people know they can count on. I love volunteers who say yes a lot. I know they won't let me down. They get the job done above and beyond what I would ever ask. I love yes people! There's also a really good chance that some of you reading this might be thinking, "I'm already really good at saying no." Hopefully, you'll take a few moments to evaluate what you're saying no to and make sure it lines up well with your priorities.

YES TO ME

I personally went through years in ministry where I felt like I could never unplug. I worked Sunday through Thursday at the church. Then Friday and Saturday I spent hours answering texts, emails, and phone calls from volunteers and parents. It was frankly disrupting my personal life. Each time I said yes to a phone call, or email, or stopped what I was doing to send a lesson through an email... again... I said no to my personal time, to taking care of my home, to investing in myself, and just resting. I wound up feeling like I was working 24/7. It became clear to me that I had to practice saying no. Is there something in your ministry right now that's taking over your personal life and disrupting your rest?

This may seem contradictory to what your pastor's heart tells you, but I want you to draw the outline of a square. It represents your personal life. Inside the square write out the pieces of your personal life that matter most. That may be: your marriage, your friendships, your kids, care of your home, time with your pets, time to write, watching your favorite TV show, or working out.

Now think about the things that interrupt your time with those people or doing the things you love. Write those things around the outside edge of the square. See that little fence there between the two sets of lists? That can be real! One of the first ways to practice your *no* is by setting up boundaries for yourself. These are not written in concrete, but they're not written in sand either. Here's what I mean: You don't have to live or die by these boundaries. There will be cases where you have to step over the line because it's an emergency, or because the volunteer is new and didn't know, or because you have a weekend event at work outside of your usual services. Don't let one little thing blow those lines away. Choose realistic boundaries for yourself. Maybe you communicate with people that on your days off you'll only check your email during certain times. Perhaps you communicate to volunteers where to look for the answers before contacting you. Or, if you serve on a team with other pastors, create a rotation of who is on call to handle these things that inevitably pop up. You figure out what works for you, but draw your lines and then communicate that well to those who need to know. Ask them to help support you in this new endeavor. The people you serve care so much about you and they know you are the very best you when you're taking time for yourself. You may be surprised at how much freedom you feel when you discover that you can go out to dinner with friends Saturday night and not dread it, knowing it'll be interrupted by a "I can't come tomorrow" text.

YES TO JUST ATTENDING... OR NOT!

Sometimes, you also have to say *no* to other church stuff. When you're on staff at a church it's easy to feel obligated to say *yes* over and over again. *Yes* to the women's retreat. *Yes* to serving at the rescue mission on Saturdays. *Yes* to re-setting chairs after an event. *Yes* to opening up the building for the baby shower rental.

Right after I started my position at StoneBridge someone came to me on a Wednesday night in the middle of programming and asked me why the door to room 113 was locked. I had no clue. I was new. I didn't even know who she was. I left my classroom of kids and unlocked it for her. Once I'd done that she told me it wasn't right. She was supposed to have a table and chairs set up. And then she just looked at me. So, I opened up the closet and drug out the table and a few chairs and set them up. I walked away feeling like I'd been run over by a dump truck. It wasn't even that unlocking the room for her or setting it up wasn't my job. It was that I didn't know how to say *no* to her. I didn't know how to prioritize the kids I was serving that night when it felt like this woman's need was pressing. This kind of situation might be hard for you too. But you are stronger when you say *no* to feeling guilty about not doing.

You are stronger when you save your *yes* for the things that are your priority. If you feel the pressure to say *yes* to everything at the church every time the doors are open, I want to release you from that right now. You've probably heard it before: You can't pour from an empty cup. There will always be one more thing. You work at a church! It's a community center, a hub for small groups, and a gathering space all week long. You simply can't be there for everything. Carefully evaluate the things that matter the most to you and give them your *yes*.

You may feel pressure from others on your church staff too. They may ask you to join in on something. They might tell you how much it would influence others if you would go. It's likely they aren't trying to guilt you into attending but rather just to let you know that they'd love to have you. Of course they would! You're a leader! And you're probably a really good time. But friends, it's okay to say *no*.

It's also okay to say *yes* and just attend. A couple of years ago I attended a women's event. Halfway through someone came into the building to set something else up. They came and got me out of the event wanting me to unlock one area and help them with something else. I had two choices: say *no* and continue attending the event or say *yes* and forfeit the event to help them set up.

You've likely been faced with a similar situation. If not, you probably will be. It's hard for people to discern when you're working and when you're attending. It's likely just as hard for them to figure it out as it is for you to figure it out. This is a great chance to practice saying *no*. I told the person at the women's event that I wasn't working that night but was there to enjoy time with other women. I handed them my key and asked them to bring it back when they were done. I left feeling so proud of myself for actually following through by simply attending that night. And guess what? The person asking for my help wasn't mad at me. They totally understood!

My friend Kristi is a yes-er. Yes-er? I know it's not a real word, but if it were, that's what she'd be. She hates to see jobs go unfinished. She doesn't like to watch others fail. She's an all-for-one and one-for-all kind of gal. She has an incredibly high level of excellence and when people from her department and others on our staff ask her to chip in, she says *yes*! She even says *yes* sometimes without being asked. She truly has a servant's heart. I'm telling you this because I know some of you are also a Kristi. You desire a win for the church and you want to do whatever it takes to make sure that happens. However, no pastor should sacrifice their family on the altar of their ministry. In the same breath, it's also important to make sure you don't sacrifice your passions (outside of ministry), your personal life, your health, your friendships, or your home on that altar either.

Ministry can be difficult to navigate. Are you going to church or are you going to work? You worship there, but you are also responsible for everything that's happening in a department that day. It's hard to pick and choose which requests to fulfill and which to turn down. Just make sure you have room to say *yes* to the things that bring you joy as well as the things that must get done. Sometimes, Kristi says *yes* because saying *yes* to that particular thing fills her bucket. She may not have time to do it, but she'll be worse off if she doesn't.

YES TO NO

I mentioned at the top of this chapter that each *yes* carries with it an equal or greater *no*. If you are a *yes* person you might be thinking, "I'm really not good at telling people *no*." And you might be right that telling other people *no* is hard for you, but I'll argue that you are, in fact, good at saying *no*. It's the reason I often remind myself that *no* is a 3-letter word. If I say *yes* to dinner and a movie with my husband, I realize I'm, in turn, saying *no* to the laundry that needs folded, or the dirty dishes by the sink, or walking the dog. It doesn't mean those things won't ever get done. It might mean they get done later. But my *yes* to date night carried a *no* alongside it to many other things. You have it in you to say *no* even if you don't feel confident or comfortable with it yet. You've been doing it all along!

You are stronger when you say *no* sometimes, but especially when it's an intentional *no* and not just a consequential *no*. This involves some real reflection. Before you give someone a hasty *yes*, evaluate what you're also saying *no* to. Are you comfortable giving those things or that person a *no*?

If you haven't already, identify some things that help you relieve stress. For me, it's easily time with my husband and friends, baking or trying a new recipe, watching TV, or working out. Once you've identified those things, make sure you're getting a healthy mix of ministry work, personal work (the adulting kinds of things like paying bills and caring for your home), and personal investment (your stress relievers). I've said *no* to serving at the rescue mission on Saturday mornings so I can get in a workout. I don't feel guilty about it. That Saturday morning workout helps me get in a good mental and physical space headed into a busy weekend of serving others.

Jesus didn't say *yes* to everything either. If He didn't, why should you? Jesus knew when He needed to say *no* to crowds and just get away for a while. Jesus said *no* when people were unfairly demanding things of Him. Jesus said *no* to baiting questions. He knew to take care of Himself. Saying *no* requires courage, so I'll leave you with these words God spoke to Joshua as he prepared to lead the Israelites and was daunted by the task at hand. *"This is my command—be strong and courageous! Do not be afraid or discouraged. For the Lord your God is with you wherever you go"* (Joshua 1:9- NLT).

It may be hard to take that first step. But just as each *yes* carries with it a *no*, you'll soon find that saying *no* sometimes allows you to say *yes* to the most life-giving things.

Aanna Smalley has served at StoneBridge Christian Church in Omaha, NE for 10 years. She loves saying "yes" to traveling with her husband, cheering on the Nebraska Cornhuskers, and Jazzercise. She loves saying "no" to decaf coffee, doing the dishes, and eating only healthy food.

chapter 10

A HEALTHY LEADER

You are stronger when you pursue health.

BY JASON BRIESACHER

I T WAS SEPTEMBER 2017 and I had an earache. My wife, two associate children's pastors, and I were getting ready to go to a conference in Texas. I didn't want to get on an airplane with an ear infection, but I hated going to the doctor. After some strong encouragement from my wife, Kathryn, I finally consented to go. Since moving to Fresno in January 2016, I had been carrying the stress of my job with me, and my wife was growing ever more concerned.

The moment I took the job, I hit the ground running. It was exhilarating. I changed systems in order to bolster our security and improve our first-time family procedures. I moved our church from a boxed curriculum into curriculum that I wrote for the ministry. I updated policies, processes, and procedures. I dealt with staff transition and conflict. I gutted our children's area and built two new worship spaces. I even started a VBS for our church. This all happened within the first six months. I don't think I slept from January until August. The only thing that kept me going were the multiple caramel macchiatos that I consumed each day. In the first year alone, my wife and I spent over $1,000 on coffee.

After that first year, I didn't slow down. I kept adding the weight of additional stresses by taking on project after project and I never unplugged. I didn't take care of myself. I carried the stress of my job and worried about numbers incessantly. I worked for weeks on end without ever taking a day off and even cancelled a family vacation. The stress of the job was with me at all times. The success I had found in my first year was nonexistent in my second year, so I doubled down and worked even harder. The weight was killing me.

I worried about my ministry and felt like I was working to keep my job. It seemed like the more I worked, the less productive I became. It wasn't just affecting my ministry, it was affecting my family and me. I gained weight every week and slept only about 4 hours each night. My hair started to hurt! Not my scalp, but my hair. It hurt to the touch. Then my ear started to hurt.

The doctor looked in my ear and saw nothing, but my ear was throbbing. My wife was with me and informed the doctor that my hair hurt. This intrigued the doctor and she figured it out almost immediately. "Shingles," she said "which is unusual for someone your age. This is usually a disease we see in men in their 60s." I was 33 and had shingles. "What could cause this?" I asked.

She explained that stress and overwork could cause shingles to present itself. I avoided looking at my wife, because I knew the look of concern she was giving me. I wasn't worried and knew that it was going to be okay, because we were leaving for a week-long conference. I could sleep, relax, and get refocused. I put all of my eggs in that basket.

Did you know that the medicine they use to treat shingles is the same one they use to treat herpes? I didn't. When the pharmacist told me that I should see my herpes clear up when I got near the end of the bottle, I freaked out. "I don't have herpes! I have shingles!" I could see the concern in the pharmacist's eyes too. "Someone your age shouldn't have shingles."

I took the medicine from the pharmacist and finished packing for Dallas. When we landed, I was prepared for relaxation, but I couldn't find it. I took a tour of the Cowboys' stadium, went to dinner with a friend, and took in some golf the next day. The whole time I thought about work or talked with people about ministry. The weight continued to crush me.

After golf, I went to the hotel and took a nap. When I woke up, something wasn't right. My face felt funny, almost like I was given Novocain. My eye was stinging and I only found relief when I pushed it closed with my hand. I couldn't close it completely. I was sure that my face would wake up and that this was only temporary.

I went to dinner with my wife and my associate children's pastors. They noticed that the right side of my face wasn't responding and was beginning to droop. I couldn't close my eye at all now and my mouth wouldn't close at the corner. I thought I was having a stroke and the look on their faces terrified me.

I called a doctor from our church and explained the situation. I told him about the shingles and my symptoms. He immediately diagnosed me with Bell's Palsy and called in a prescription over the phone. He explained that the shingles had touched a nerve in my face and had seized them. It would take time for my system to reboot and would take some effort to strengthen my face again. He recommended steroids to strengthen my facial muscles and an eye patch to keep my eye closed.

I was embarrassed. I would have to go to a conference looking like a pirate. He told me that I would have to wear the eye patch for about six weeks. I knew I would have to go home and wear it to church. I was mortified. Then, I had to experience the conference. The pitiful looks I received from people were, I'm sure, magnified by my own humiliation. I tried to make the best of the situation but was so angry and upset. Each session and breakout made it worse. In a breakout, I was asked to take a whistle and blow it as my teammates played a game. I couldn't wrap my mouth around the whistle. In our large group sessions, I couldn't sing to God. My mouth wasn't responding the way it should.

I was irritated at God. "I'm doing this for You." While my intention was to do this for Him, killing myself with work and creating an unhealthy lifestyle was not what God wanted for my life or my leadership.

That was a wake-up call for me and I pulled back from work. I decided to honor my days off and tried not to stress about work. While the eye patch and slurred words were embarrassing, it didn't force me to change my lifestyle. I still drank too much coffee, grabbed snack items instead of eating meals, and didn't sleep. I tried to get more sleep, but I had trained my body to operate on 4 hours a day and I woke up in the middle of the night ready to go. I felt worse. Because I couldn't sleep, I stressed about sleep. My blood pressure rose steadily.

When you lack sleep, you can't function at your best. A lack of sleep slows you down physically, mentally, and puts your emotions on edge. A sleepless person is like an exposed nerve—the slightest movement could set them off. Dr. Merrill Mitler, a sleep expert and neuroscientist at the National Institute of Health, wrote that a "loss of sleep impairs your higher levels of reasoning, problem-solving and attention to detail. Tired people tend to be less productive at work. They're at a much higher risk for traffic accidents. Lack of sleep also influences your mood, which can affect how you interact with others. A sleep deficit over time can even put you at greater risk for developing depression." ("The Benefits of Slumber", News in Health) Do you wake up foggy? Do you require caffeine to function? These are signs that you need to get more sleep. Sleep will make you a better leader. It will help you think, function, and react appropriately. In the middle of this crisis, I was not thinking, functioning, or reacting appropriately, but a friend reached out to help.

This friend was my executive pastor, Brad. He was concerned. In our weekly meeting, I asked him what my goals should be for the upcoming year. His answer was not ministry related at all. He said, "Jason, my goal for you in the next year is for you to become the best version of yourself—the healthiest person—so that you can be a good dad, a good husband, and a good pastor. If you don't, you're not going to make it. If you focus on becoming the best version of yourself, you will be amazed how your work life will improve."

I was upset. This is not a tangible goal I could reach out and touch. If he told me to come up with five new initiatives or read 100 books, I would do it. How do I measure whether or not I'm becoming a better husband, father, or person? I was irritated with his request. Doesn't he know the stress I'm under trying to make this ministry successful?

I left the meeting and thought about what he said. Brad had been investing in me since before he hired me as the children's pastor. He had been an amazing mentor. He took care of my family like no other leader had before. Brad involved himself deeply in the lives of each member of my family and he genuinely cared about their well-being.

Knowing how much he cared for me and my family, I wasn't going to shrink away from his challenge. I began to force myself to sleep at night, but couldn't get to sleep before 2am. I took sleeping aids to help me go to bed earlier and sleep longer, but it didn't work. Sleep was still elusive; I didn't know what to do. I knew I couldn't go on like this much longer. My dream of being a children's pastor was slipping through my fingers, because I couldn't sleep nor could I shake off the stress. Something needed to change.

My wife and I decided to try to lose some weight together. I hoped that losing weight would help me find sleep. We shifted our eating patterns and kept each other accountable. I made sure that I ate regularly. Creating new habits was miserable, but sleep was easier to find after I lost 10 pounds. After I lost 30 pounds, my body drifted off to sleep very easily. If you want to cut out stress and find your sleep, lose weight.

Most people in ministry do not eat regular meals. You're moving from one meeting to another and from one project to another. Eating regularly can prevent hunger pains, boost metabolism, energize you, and help encourage self-control, all while you create new habits. ("Why is it important to eat meals at regular times?" *Tru Health Medicine*) Eat three portioned meals each day and three snacks, about 100 calories each, between them. And drink water.

We drank, and still drink, a lot of water. You should be drinking at least 64 ounces of water daily and talk with your doctor about building it up to half your body weight in ounces. As much as sleep benefits your body, water does as well. According to James McIntosh from *Medical News Today*, water lubricates your joints, delivers oxygen, and cushions your bones, brain, spinal cord, and nervous system. It regulates your body temperature, aids in digestion, and flushes waste. It lowers your blood pressure and increases your accessible nutrients. ("Fifteen Benefits of Drinking Water") Water is the fuel your body needs to function.

I learned to listen to my body. According to the Polycystic Kidney Disease Foundation, human beings have difficulty distinguishing between hunger and thirst. "Most people confuse thirst and hunger, often mistaking the former for the latter. Clinical studies have shown that 37% of people mistake hunger for thirst" ("Hunger Versus Thirst", *PKD*). You aren't giving your body what it needs because you're misunderstanding the signals. You think you're hungry, so you eat. Your body needs water and is calling out for it. If you want to lose weight, start drinking water.

I had to force myself to create new habits and goals. I had to be honest with my wife and stay on our new plan together. After the first few weeks, I lost 10 pounds. I was motivated and set some ambitious goals. I shared them with friends so I could stay accountable to them. I walked home from work, most days, which is about two miles. This allowed me to exercise and, more importantly, decompress from the day before I got home to try and be a husband and father. That 30 to 45-minute walk home was refreshing mentally and invigorating physically. It helped me shed more weight as well.

After a few more weeks, I was down 30 pounds. As I shed the weight, something amazing happened: I found sleep! As I found sleep, my blood pressure dropped. As my blood pressure dropped, my stress level dropped. When my stress level dropped, I was able to function without needing coffee several times each day. I found my frustrations decreased and my patience increased. My decision-making improved.

My brain became clearer as I pursued health. I found my creativity returning and new ideas forming. The weight fell off of both of us. As of today, I've lost almost 70 pounds and my wife has lost 60 pounds. Sleep is not elusive; it finds me each night. I sleep through the night without waking up and, for the first time in years, I wake up feeling refreshed.

In the last few months, I've started more initiatives. I've challenged myself to dream and empower more, to delegate more, and to live in the big picture of our ministry. I have pared down my job to the 2 or 3 things that only I can do and have delegated the rest. I've recruited more volunteers in the last few months than I did in the previous year. I dream about how we can impact parents, grandparents, and families so that we can transform the lives of kids. Before, I was fighting to survive. Now, I can thrive.

Previously, I made so many decisions, both about my life and ministry, based on my self-esteem and self-perspective. I said for years that I didn't like to dance, but that was directly related to how I felt about myself. Now, I enjoy dancing with the kids. It's fun!

I'm so thankful that my leader pushed me to pursue the best version of me. Pursuing health has improved my quality of life which made me a better leader. Pursuing health made me a better husband and father. Pursuing health made me stronger.

My pursuit of health was only possible because I decided to be honest with myself, evaluate and assess my situation, and then respond. You can pursue health by following those same steps. H.E.A.R. what God is saying to you about how your body and ministry work together.

H – HONEST

Be honest with yourself about how you're feeling. There are only two people who know when you're not being honest with yourself: you and God. Talk with Him about how you can improve your health, lose weight, and get better sleep. What if you made health as big of a priority as leadership development? Pursuing health will make you a better leader. Jim Wideman said that if he were to go back in time and talk to a younger version of himself, he would encourage him to take better care of his health.

Honesty will help you create a plan that will lead you from where you are to where God wants you to be. Honesty will help you look in the mirror and see the areas in which you need to improve.

E – EVALUATE

Evaluation needs to be multi-faceted. You should evaluate your workload, activities, and responsibilities. When looking over your workload, there might be 10 things you're really good at, but how many of those must be done by you? There are probably only 2 or 3 things that only you can do.

One of the reasons I didn't pursue health for so long was that I was busy doing and not busy leading. Your job is to equip the saints for the work of ministry (Ephesians 4:12). There is only so much time in the week and only so much you can hold on your plate.

Pursuing health must be a priority; only you can lose your weight. Only you can exercise for you. Only you can change your eating plan. No one can fix your health for you, but someone else could come up with crafts or make videos. Someone else could take on that Wednesday night program. What are things that you're doing that could be done by someone else? What can only be done by you?

If you are to pursue health, you have to create time for it. If you never create time, you will never have time. Set aside time to walk every night and read every morning. This will improve your body and mind. Consistently evaluate your weight, measurements, caloric intake, exercise, and water consumption. Make a plan that you can follow and share your plan with others for accountability.

A - ASSESS

If you are going to create time to pursue health, you can't simply give everything away at once. Delegation without review is abandonment. Don't evaluate and shed all your responsibilities all at once. This is a multi-step process. Shedding your responsibilities will follow the same pattern you'll need to follow when pursuing health. Make a change and then evaluate. Delegate some responsibility to a volunteer and then evaluate. Help them be successful by encouraging them along the way. You will see how amazing they can be and how much it frees you to do the things that only you can do. You didn't gain weight all at once and you're not going to lose it all at once. You need to shed some of your responsibilities so that you have the margin to pursue health.

During this time, it's important to assess whether or not changes are working. Remember, the number on the scale doesn't necessarily indicate that your methods are working or not. You may be losing inches, but not losing weight as quickly. Don't be discouraged! This journey of weight loss begins with the first step.

R – RESPOND

This is where the rubber meets the road. This is a long journey that begins with a first step. Create margin in your life so that you can pursue health. Practice self-control and change your eating habits as you create margin. Shed responsibilities so you can add exercise into your daily routine. Change your schedule and make sleep a priority. Drink water throughout the day and eat regularly. You'll find your weight and your stress falling off as you pursue the healthiest version of yourself.

I encourage you to take a moment, right now, and add these three things to your schedule for this upcoming month and see how you feel:

1. Read in the morning
2. Drink water throughout the day
3. Walk at night.

This only worked for me because I decided to listen to the advice of a friend. I'm reaching out to you today, as a friend, and I'm asking you to H.E.A.R. this advice and heed it. Only you can make these changes in order to transform yourself into the strongest possible leader. You are a better leader when you improve yourself. You are a smarter leader when you make these changes. You are a stronger leader when you pursue health.

Jason Briesacher is passionate about two things: teaching kids about Jesus and empowering leaders to create environments where the Gospel can be shared effectively. Jason has served at mega-churches, church plants, and is currently at Peoples Church in Fresno, CA, implementing his practical ministry ideas weekly.

chapter 11

WILL WE BE NAKED IN HEAVEN?

You are stronger when you continue to learn.

BY TERESA D. WELCH

MISS TERESA! MISS TERESA!"

"Yes. Nathan?"

"I have a question."

Approximately 40 elementary-aged children were settling into the kids' worship space when 11-year-old Nathan remembered the question he had been waiting several days to ask me.

"Go ahead. What is your question?"

"Since Adam and Eve were naked in the Garden of Eden..."

Younger kids started to giggle at hearing the word "naked."

"And heaven is supposed to be like the Garden of Eden..."

Before he could even get the words out of his mouth, I knew where this was going.

"Does that mean we will be naked in heaven?"

Nathan beamed from ear to ear. Kids burst out in laughter. Volunteers covered their mouths to control their snickers. And I was hit with a wave of emotions all at once. Surprise at the question. Panic to regain control of the room. And pride. Pride that "one of my kids" was putting all of the pieces together.

I had been fortunate to learn specific tools of children's ministry to handle that particular moment. Classroom management taught me how to regain control of the room and transition from giggles to worship. Age-level development taught me that Nathan was demonstrating cognitive growth. But I was also fortunate to have learned something else that was helpful in that moment. I knew the answer to his question.

If you have been in kidmin leadership for any length of time, you have had a Nathan moment. A hand goes up, a child asks a question, and you are on the spot to respond to something that was definitely not part of your lesson plan. But these are not the only moments when you can be put on the spot. A parent approaches you with a question about applying a confusing scripture. A volunteer asks for historical or cultural background on a story that their teaching materials didn't include. Do you feel equipped to answer their question or find the answer?

The story of Timothy has always captured my attention. Perhaps you too memorized the verse of encouragement written to him by Paul, *"Don't let anyone look down on you because you are young, but set an example for the believers in speech, in conduct, in love, in faith and in purity"* (1 Timothy 4:12, NIV). Paul entrusted a young Timothy with the leadership of the church at Ephesus. Timothy's preparation to lead did not begin when he was a young adult or teenager. Instead, Timothy had been equipped to preach and teach the Word of God from his birth. Paul's final charge to Timothy says, *"But as for you, continue in what you have learned and have become convinced of, because you know those from whom you learned it, and how from infancy you have known the Holy Scriptures, which are able to make you wise for salvation through faith in Christ Jesus"* (2 Timothy 3:14-15, NIV). It is earlier in the letter that Paul reveals the identity of Timothy's first teachers: his grandmother Lois and mother Eunice (2 Timothy 1:5, NIV).

These knowledgeable women passed down more than the stories of faith to Timothy. They equipped him with the Word of God. Lois and Eunice guided Timothy to *become convinced of* the power of the Gospel to save. Notice Paul's admonition to Timothy: *"Continue in what you have learned."* Paul goes on to say, *"All Scripture is God-breathed and is useful for teaching, rebuking, correcting, and training in righteousness, so that the servant of God may be thoroughly equipped for every good work"* (2 Timothy 3:16-17, NIV). The instruction of Paul to Timothy is one that you who teach, rebuke, correct, and train children should follow. Continue in what you have learned so that you can pass on the faith to those who follow you, so that they, in turn, can train others in the faith.

CONTINUE IN WHAT YOU HAVE LEARNED

You balance these roles: schedule organizer, volunteer recruiter, parent counselor, and event planner. But your role also includes: interpreter of scripture, training young Bible scholars; theologian, shaping the understanding of curiosity seekers; church historian, pointing kids toward understanding their place in the story of God; and spiritual director, guiding children in their growing faith. In order to play these important roles, you must continue in what you have learned.

Interpreting scripture

No matter how long you've been walking with Christ and serving in kidmin, there's always more to know and understand about the Word of God. Learning the tools of biblical

interpretation, including historical, cultural, and literary context, equips you to answer questions. Preparation for teaching should include information beyond what you will use in
your lesson, because that knowledge enhances your teaching.
Just last week, 9-year-old Drake raised his hand at the end
of a lesson on the building of Solomon's Temple and asked,
"Is the Temple still standing?" In short, the answer is no.
But instead of the short answer, I took time to connect the
Temple Solomon built to stories he had learned about Daniel
in Babylon, Nehemiah rebuilding Jerusalem, Jesus in the
Temple at age 12, and the crucifixion of Christ.

The tools of biblical interpretation also equip you to train
young students how to interpret the Bible. Children have
the ability to do more than learn the books of the Bible or
locate scripture texts. Train them to use Bible study tools
(concordances, maps, Bible dictionaries), to study the use
of biblical words in scripture, to compare parallel texts, and
to draw connections between the Old and New Testaments.
Introduce them to Hebrew and Greek words to help them
understand the unique vocabulary of the Bible. Guide kids,
parents, and volunteers to resources that will assist them in
finding the answers to their questions, equipping them for
further study.

Church doctrine and theology

Knowledge of biblical interpretation is the place to start, but
your learning should not stop there. Studying church doctrine
and theology helps apply scripture to life. Have you ever had a
child ask you: Why did God allow Adam and Eve to sin? Why
does God allow bad things to happen? Is my grandma in heav-
en? Answering these questions is never easy. Understanding
theology, eschatology, and all those other "-ology" words gives
you the tools to guide kids and parents in faith conversations.
The study of doctrine helps you understand your church's tradition alongside the application of scripture around the world.

This can give you the confidence to evaluate curriculum from various publishers and identify the adjustments you need to make when your church's doctrine does not align with the materials provided.

Church history and tradition

Ever wonder why some churches baptize infants, some baptize children around ages 5 or 6, and others around age 12 or 13? What do you believe about the nature of an infant born into the world? Are they innately sinful, a blank slate, or innately good? Understanding church history and how the church has approached the education of children helps you better understand your tradition and others. As you welcome families into your church, they may bring with them a different Christian heritage. With that heritage comes questions about why and how your church is different. The tradition of churches to which I belong practices baptism when an individual demonstrates accountability for their actions, belief in Christ, and repentance of sin. An understanding of church history and traditions has helped me answer questions and concerns from parents and grandparents about the difference in our practice of baptism, as well as other rituals of the church.

Spiritual disciplines

Scripture, theology, and church history are not the only tools in raising young disciples. It is never too young for a child to begin daily spiritual habits of prayer and worship. But each child is unique and needs individual guidance in their faith formation. For example, Nathan demonstrated in his question he was ready for certain conversations in faith development, while others his age were not. As children learn to pray and worship, you are like the priest Eli to young Samuel (1 Samuel 3), helping them recognize the voice of the Lord. Your knowledge of the spiritual disciplines and the work of the Lord in faith formation equips you to guide these kids towards becoming convinced of the Word of God.

RESOURCES TO CONTINUE YOUR LEARNING

Each kidmin leader has a limit of resources at their disposal, including time and finances, to continue their learning. But for every situation, there are resources to help you along your journey.

Higher Education Institutions: Courses, Programs, and Resources

I'm a children's minister turned college professor, so I'll admit, I have a bias. But, I think one of the best ways for children's ministry leaders to continue learning is with an institution of biblical higher education. Most denominations and affiliation of churches have their own colleges, universities, or seminaries for the purpose of biblical and theological education. Some denominations have undergraduate Bible colleges or Christian universities where students can earn a bachelor's degree in biblical studies and professional ministry. Others require an undergraduate degree in any field to provide a breadth of education before entering graduate studies at a seminary for theological and ministerial training. With the growth of online education, many institutions offer courses and degree programs that do not require you to relocate for school, so you can continue serving in your current ministry.

If you're interested in this avenue of learning, several resources can guide you in locating places for continuing education. The College Navigator for the National Center for Educational Statistics (nces.ed.gov/collegenavigator) allows prospective students to search for schools based on various characteristics, including region of the country and denominational affiliation. The websites for the Council for Christian Colleges and Universities (cccu.org), the Association of Theological Schools (ats.edu), and the Association for Biblical Higher Education (abhe.org) provide lists of accredited schools with biblical and theological education programs.

Whether you can pursue a degree or just take a few courses, continuing your education has both immediate and long-term benefits for your leadership in kidmin. It was my third year as a children's minister when the church I served entered into a season of conflict. The result was that the church split right down the middle. I was ready to walk away from ministry. However, I was fortunate that one night a week I met with a community of classmates and professors at a nearby graduate school. They encouraged me, advised me, and sustained me. If it were not for them, I don't think I would have entered a fourth year of children's ministry, let alone my 25th year. Sit in a classroom or meet online with others training for ministry and you will be encouraged. This becomes a place for community and connection for you outside your ministry setting.

But maybe you don't have either the time or financial resources to enroll in college or seminary. If you can't enroll to pursue a degree, don't remove Christian colleges and seminaries from your list for consideration. Higher education institutions provide resources for churches and individuals at low or no cost. Search college websites in your region for their schedule of lectureships, seminars, conferences, and weekly chapel services. Look at college and seminary websites for online resources, such as blogs, podcasts, or videos their faculty produce to provide continued training for their alumni and community. Also consider auditing a course. An audited course won't count toward earning a degree, but the cost of the course is less and you don't have to do the homework.

Create your own path of study: Publishing Houses and Libraries

Another path for learning is to create your own course of study. Ask your lead pastor, college professors, or others in kidmin leadership to recommend books and resources. Look at the Academic Resources section of the websites of Christian publishers for the textbooks that colleges and seminaries use. Publishing houses also provide online materials that supplement their textbooks. These materials are similar to online courses and can be completed at your own pace of learning. If you need a place to start, read *How to Read the Bible for All Its Worth*. (Gordon D. Fee and Douglas Stuart) This resource provides a good foundation for biblical interpretation and a starting point for your own path of study.

Don't forget to consider the resources at your local public or college library. Ask the library staff for help in finding resources at their library or through online databases. Many libraries have access to resources from other libraries in their region, including theological libraries. Preparing to teach a Christmas or Easter series? Check out a few Bible commentaries on the gospels of Matthew and Luke. Walking through stories of the Old Testament? There are a variety of Bible dictionaries that provide helpful overviews of biblical books, background on characters, and descriptions of Bible locations. Preparing to study a word like love, belief, or salvation with kids? There are various resources that provide information to help define the use of the word in scripture.

Whether you're new to kidmin leadership or have been on the journey for a while, it's never too early or too late to continue in your learning.

ANSWERING THE QUESTION

When 11-year-old Nathan asked the question that day, my training and experience in classroom management helped me redirect the class to the topic for the day. My knowledge of cognitive development helped me recognize that he was transitioning from concrete to abstract thinking and had made new mental connections. It was my education in biblical and theological studies, along with the work of the Holy Spirit, that equipped me to answer his question that morning.

"Great question, Nathan! The book of Revelation describes heaven. This book was written by John, one of the 12 disciples of Jesus, who wrote down a vision he had of heaven. According to John, people in heaven are dressed in white robes. White robes represent that the blood of Christ forgives our sins and makes us holy and perfect. So, in other words, we will be wearing special clothes in heaven!" (Notice I didn't say the word *naked* again. Twice was enough!)

Fortunately, the learning for Nathan didn't stop there. It opened the door for more questions and the discovery of more answers together. Kids like Nathan encourage me *to continue in what I had learned* so that like Lois and Eunice, I can lead them to be convinced of the truth and prepare them for leadership.

KidMin Nation is stronger when you continue in what you have learned.

Teresa D. Welch (Bachelor of Christian Education, Master of Arts in Family and Youth Ministry, Master of Divinity, Doctor of Ministry) After being "Miss Teresa" for 15 years as a children's minister in Ohio and Illinois, she also became "Dr. Welch" serving for 10 years as a college and seminary professor. Teresa currently has the best of two worlds as she trains students at Ozark Christian College for ministry (Joplin, MO) and serves as a volunteer alongside a great kidmin team at Carterville Christian Church.

chapter 12

THRIVING, NO MATTER WHAT!

I am stronger when I know how to handle conflict.

BY AMY GOBLE

HAVE YOU EVER EXPERIENCED conflict at your church? Maybe the better question is: Can you remember a time when you were not in conflict at your church? Conflict can quickly work its way into situations where you work with teams. In fact, 40% of pastors report a serious conflict with a church member at least once a month. ("Pastor Stress Statistics", soulshepherding.org) So, what if you had the ability to handle conflict skillfully? What if you could prevent conflict from exploding? What if conflict did not have to be crippling but could actually make you stronger?

What if one of the goals of handling conflict is to teach you to be more resilient? To be resilient simply means "to be able to withstand or recover quickly from difficult conditions." Does this sound like what you would like to be? It is possible, and you can begin to see each conflict as another chance to practice building strength and resiliency.

Learning to handle conflict can be a life-long endeavor. The goal of this chapter is to get you started with practical things you can do when faced with conflict. Let's look at two ways to build resiliency in you and your team, and to grow stronger in your conflict resolution skills.

PREVENTION

Perhaps you've heard the old saying, "What is the best way to get out of hot water? To never get in it in the first place!" The good news is there are great ways you can get in front of conflict so it rarely has to happen. You can prevent conflict from erupting. The next time you're in a situation that can lead to conflict, ask these questions.

Have you communicated effectively?

Imagine sitting in staff meeting as a new event is being discussed. It occurs to you that this event is not going to work for the kids' ministry schedule. In fact, this event is going to really push your volunteers over the edge. You want to say something, but decide against it. In the months that follow, you are in multiple intense moments and arguments as you try to protect your volunteers at that event.

Now imagine again, you're sitting in that same staff meeting as a new event is being discussed. This time, as soon as you realize it's not in the best interest of your team, you raise your hand to share your concerns and creative ideas on how they can be addressed. The difference this time is that those in the meeting have a chance to respond to your concerns and design an event that meets everyone's needs. After hearing your concerns, they may still choose to go forward with the original plan. Even if they do choose to move forward, it's now on record how the kids' ministry could flourish in this event.

Communicating clearly will lay a framework that you can build on in later conversations.

Can you overlook it?

This is not a popular question to ask! Let's look at Scripture: *"... it is to one's glory to overlook an offense"* (Proverbs 19:11b, NIV). In other words, if you can simply say, "I am not going to let it bother me," and walk away, please do. Most conflicts can be avoided by moving on and not letting it bother you. I wonder if, right now, you're thinking this is too hard to do. Remember, you actually do this all the time! Can you imagine how angry you would be if you got truly upset each time a child interrupted you while you were trying to teach? That could be many times on a typical Sunday morning! Or if you lost your mind every time a volunteer did something crazy? Stop and think about it; there are multiple times a day that you simply keep walking when conflict presents itself. So, when you're in an intense situation, if possible, try to move on and not allow an offense to take root.

What are your assumptions?

Everyone does it! Human beings make a lot of assumptions. For example, you assume that the restaurant where you're eating has cleaned their kitchen and prepared the food properly. You assume that the people on the road will stay in their lane, and you assume the email you sent will go to the right person. However, assumptions can also be the main cause behind your conflict.

A few years ago, I was really mad at our student pastor. He kept dumping his work onto my plate. It put me over the edge when he announced in staff meeting that he was starting a new ministry for preteens. I had announced the previous week that I was going to be the one to start a ministry for preteens! As you can imagine, I was furious. Instead of talking with him about it, I huffed off and stopped talking to him altogether. I wanted nothing to do with him and I assumed that he was trying to invade and undermine the children's ministry.

A few months later, we both agreed to a lunch meeting to discuss the new preteen ministry. I told him how mad I was and that the pastor had asked me to start the preteen ministry. Guess what? He was floored! You see, the pastor had asked him to start the preteen ministry, too! We were both mad at each other for stepping on each other's toes and it was not even what happened! We had a great laugh when we realized that it was our pastor who had given us this information! Once we realized what happened (and stopped assuming the worst about each other), we talked with our pastor and split the preteen ministry up into age-appropriate areas. It was a fabulous ending! Remember this question the next time you sense conflict: What are you assuming about the other person/about why they are doing what they are doing? See if you can determine what story or assumptions you are believing and fact check with the other person before you decide how to respond.

Are you ignoring signs of trouble?

I'm not just talking about the big stuff (like stealing or lying). I'm talking about pushing past that little feeling you get when you know something is not quite right. It's those times when the Holy Spirit is talking to you and you get a check in your spirit to choose a different path, even if it's not obvious to others. A while ago, I had a staff member who reported to me. He seemed really talented. I knew when we brought him on that he could be emotional; however, I was sure I could handle it. Over the years of working together, little things emerged that were concerning. I handed him contact information for new volunteers and yet never saw them volunteer on Sunday mornings. When asked about it, he said he tried to contact them yet never heard back. He kept telling us that no one wanted to serve in kids' ministry, and he must have a team of hired staff. I thought that was odd, but I pushed past the feeling that something was not adding up. Later, in a new building project, I asked about adding a new check-in system. He said our pastor had not approved it. That didn't sound like my pastor, so I asked him about it. He actually had approved it. Again, I did nothing. I pushed past the feeling that something was off. Finally, we ended up with multiple teams that would not talk with the rest of the church. They were so afraid of what would happen if he became emotional and were too scared to tell us what was happening. I was devastated. I can now look back and see all the times the Holy Spirit tried to tell me something was wrong, and I ignored it.

So, if you get that feeling in your spirit that something is off, listen! Listen to what God is trying to tell you. Do not push past that sense of caution. Take the time to pray it through and search it out.

What do you want to create?

This question has the ability to change your life! When you find yourself in an uncomfortable situation, ask yourself (or them): What do you want to create? This takes the focus off of what is wrong and puts the focus onto what is possible. I've seen this work over and over again. First, what kind of environment do you want to create in your ministry? In your volunteer teams? In your staff meetings? Do you want to create a place of trust where everyone feels safe and they can learn and grow? Do you want a place where they are inspired and elevated to be able to grow in their leadership? Then, you can begin creating that environment. It doesn't happen overnight, but knowing where you're heading and what you want to create will move you in the right direction each time! Second, if you're in the heat of conflict and you stop long enough to ask the person you're talking with, "What do you want to create?", you can arrive at a shared goal or discover what's really important to the other person. It's a way to get to the bottom of what they're trying to accomplish so you can accomplish those goals together.

You Have a Choice

Well, it finally happened. You did everything that you could to be agreeable and you are now in the midst of a giant conflict. This unpleasant situation could be with a volunteer, another staff member, or even your pastor. I used to think if I behaved myself and stayed in my children's ministry lane that blow-out fights could not happen to me. Wow, I was wrong. It all started with my attending a conference. Things were going great, my co-worker and I were on a good stride, partnering together whenever possible and enjoying life. After the conference, I returned to my church ready to share what I had learned, only to find out that my co-worker had moved offices. Strange, huh? I thought it was no big deal until the other staff members approached me and asked me why I had treated our co-worker so poorly. I quickly learned that he had spent the week I was away spreading rumors about me. I was caught off guard and hurt. I asked myself all the questions above and was ready to talk with him and work it out. He refused. He literally would not talk or communicate with me in any way.

So, what do you do when you're in conflict, you want to handle it biblically and appropriately, yet that's not possible? Remember, you have a choice! In these situations, you always have the ability to deal with you. You might not be able to deal or communicate with others, but you can deal with your own heart. You get to choose forgiveness or bitterness. You get to choose staying hurt or moving forward. You get to choose if you give up mental space, rehashing what happened, or if you live in peace. Don't get me wrong, this is not easy. But the more you do it, the easier it will get. You are not a victim. You have the God-given ability to choose to move forward, even in the most difficult situations, in forgiveness and peace.

One of the best things about conflict is learning that you do not have to label it "bad." You can learn a lot about yourself and a lot about God from walking through a conflict. Does this seem impossible? All the hard situations and conflicts that I've mentioned in this chapter are something that I would not trade for anything. I have learned so much about what God can do in my heart and how to be a better leader from these experiences. Each time you find yourself experiencing a trying situation, start to look for the good, knowing that God works everything together for the good and He can be fully trusted. Ask yourself this question, "What is the gift of God to me in this?" If you can't quite see it yet, relax in the fact that God is in control and He will bring something good from it. With God's help, you can walk through conflict and emerge stronger, happier, and full of joy. Remember God's promise, *"I am certain that God, who began the good work within you, will continue his work until it is finally finished on the day when Christ Jesus returns"* (Philippians 1:6, NLT).

Amy Goble is the Elementary Children's Pastor at Bear Valley Church and the founder of KidsPray.tv. Amy loves hanging out with her family, movies, and going to Disney World. She appreciates great Mexican food and a well-organized event!

chapter 13

GOD WINS!

You are stronger when you delegate.

BY BUTCH HUNTER

THE CHURCH OFFICES were all empty. It was one of those late nights no one looked forward to. Exhausted and lonely, Brian sat at his desk. He felt like the weight of the world had been dumped on him. A large task list lay before him, taunting him, sending his frazzled emotions into overdrive.

Resting his head in the palms of his hands, he stared down at the list. He had just been put in charge of a new church-wide outreach event with a short deadline. It was an important family-focused event, designed to establish closer relationships in the church while reaching out to the surrounding community to share the love of Jesus with those unfamiliar with the young church.

A hastily assembled team had met together earlier in the evening. The atmosphere had been positive, and the group generated exciting ideas. Now Brian was left to bring it together, in addition to his normal work duties, which were becoming overwhelming as the church grew. His thoughts raced. How can I pull this off? Where do I even start? He began to pray, asking God for wisdom.

Does Brian's situation resonate with you?

Believe it or not, one of the Bible's greatest leaders found himself in a very similar situation. In Exodus 18, we're told that Moses became weary with the never-ending task list that accompanied the job of shepherding God's people after leading them out of Egypt. As the Israelites wandered from place to place, Moses spent most of his time ruling over the many disputes that came up among the people. Two million people can generate a lot of disputes! Talk about exhausting! Moses' father-in-law, Jethro, watched what was happening, and he realized Moses was fading fast. God gave Jethro the wisdom to understand that Moses couldn't continue to shoulder the overwhelming responsibility of judging every petty case brought before him. Jethro advised Moses to share his responsibilities with other trusted leaders who could report back to him. In other words, Jethro urged Moses to delegate certain jobs before he wore himself out.

After Brian poured his heart out to God, he opened his eyes and looked around his office—a typical children's pastor's office filled with props, prizes, toys, and books. Brian noticed a stack of kids' movie posters he was collecting for an upcoming series. As he thumbed through the pile, he realized these kids' movies had something to teach about leadership. (It's amazing what you can learn from kids' movies!)

The Incredibles, Toy Story, A Bug's Life, Cars. Every movie told the story of a group of characters facing a dilemma or a job in need of completion. Every movie also revealed the story of a leader who rallied his troops to get the job done. Instead of Lone Rangers, the movies portrayed leaders who were able to pull out the best in their team members—leaders who saw potential, unique skills, value, and importance in others. Flick, Woody, Lightning McQueen—they pulled the best from individuals to make their teams stronger.

As Brian continued to contemplate the leadership principles of some of his favorite cartoon characters, he realized that he couldn't be a Lone Ranger anymore. God had listened to his heart's call. In the stillness of Brian's desperation, God answered his prayer for wisdom. God made it clear that Brian needed to delegate some of his responsibilities.

Delegation is one of the most important leadership practices you will ever use. How you delegate can literally make or break your ministry. Jethro's advice to Moses was simple and straightforward: find a team of people to be in charge of others. Sounds easy enough, right? Not so fast. Good delegation requires planning, discernment, prayer, and continued oversight.

FIRST THINGS FIRST—START WITH A TASK LIST

You can't delegate if you don't know exactly what needs to be done. This is where you break up your larger vision into smaller, more manageable pieces. Start by creating a basic list of tasks to be accomplished. You could also make a list of ministry categories, like preschool, elementary, worship, and drama. If you're planning an event, your categories might include hospitality, parking, set-up, clean-up, and food. Think of this list as a set of job descriptions.

People succeed when they take ownership of a project, and people take ownership when they are fully equipped and clear on direction. Job descriptions should include the following information: estimated time commitment, methods of communication, meeting schedules, role expectations, resources, training materials, budget, and any other pertinent information.

Moses assigned his judges different levels of delegation. Some judges were appointed over groups of 10, some were given groups of 50, others 100s, and still others 1,000s. Items on your list will require different levels of commitment. Some assignments will be short-term; others may be more complicated or require a longer time commitment. You must be able to clearly articulate the expectations of each role.

HONESTLY ASSESS YOURSELF

This step requires humility and honesty. What are your strengths and weaknesses? What are your limits? Are there tasks on this list that only you can do? You'll find that there are some jobs that can only be done by you; those are the assignments you must do. On the other hand, there may be things you like to do, but is there someone else who could do them just as easily, or maybe even better than you? You might need to really wrestle with this evaluation. Don't let ego or pride get in the way of an honest look at yourself. Be willing to let go of things, even if you love doing them.

Moses was called to teach the people God's Law, and serve as the go-between with God and the people, while casting God's vision for the young nation of Israel. God hand-picked Moses to handle these huge responsibilities. No one else could do them. The judges were given reign over smaller issues, but they still brought the most difficult cases to Moses. This freed Moses to do the things that only he could do. Good delegation gives you time and energy to do the things that only you can do.

PARTNER WITH GOD BY PRAYING SPECIFICALLY

Now that you have a list, and you've decided what needs to be handed off, start praying specifically for individuals who can come alongside you to help you accomplish the vision God has given you. Pray that God will help you become aware of people as individuals with their own strengths, gifts, and talents. Pray that those with the gifting and skill sets needed will be attracted to your ministry, and that your ministry will become a place where others can joyfully serve God.

INTENTIONALLY LOOK FOR INDIVIDUALS

Moses didn't wait for volunteers to come to him. He chose men from throughout Israel to become judges. After you pray, go out and talk with people. Find out where their hearts are leading them, and how they think God is calling them to serve. Hold a class to help people discover their spiritual gifting and present them with opportunities to serve on your team.

Make a list of those currently serving in your ministry. You will probably see potential in many of them that they don't see themselves. One time at a new ministry, I "inherited" a volunteer who served in the nursery. It was clear to just about everybody that she highly disliked her position, but she wouldn't give it up. I noticed that she did seem to enjoy organizing the nursery supplies each week, and that sparked an idea. The children's ministry resource room was a chaotic mess in need of some good organization. To make a long story short, this wonderful volunteer who was unhappy in her role, decided to take on that resource room challenge after we had coffee together one day. She loved her new duties, cheerfully took ownership, and our resource room became a useful, organized space. She was happier, and the ministry became stronger as she continued to manage our resource room.

I want to mention one thing here. Don't ever just look for bodies to fill a space. You may solve your problem in the short run, but you'll only create trouble for later. Jethro mentioned several specific qualifications for the judges. First, he mentioned that they be capable. He also required a fear of God, trustworthiness, and a moral opposition to accepting bribes. Since you are responsible for children, you have a great obligation to surround them with Christ-like people.

As you work through this step, you might find that some people are better suited to ministry in other areas of the church, not the children's ministry. Don't be afraid to let them go because you need volunteers. Be gracious in letting them serve in a place where they'll bloom.

KEEP IN CONTACT WITH YOUR TEAM

Delegation doesn't mean giving up responsibility. I remember an old preacher friend who posted a sign outside his office door that read, "The buck stops here." As the leader of a thriving church, he knew the importance of delegating, but he also recognized that the ultimate responsibility belonged to him as God's appointed pastor of that flock. The hard truth is that you are responsible for your ministry area. Recognize and accept that responsibility.

Delegating can be risky. Because you are responsible for the outcome in your ministry, you need to keep track of what's going on without micro-managing. Keep in regular contact with your team members encouraging them, trouble-shooting with them, and celebrating victories with them. Schedule time together as a group for brainstorming, building comradeship, and tightening up the details. Your coaching will play a huge part in your team's level of success.

Delegation makes your ministry strong when it's done well. It enables you to spend your time on the things that only you can do, while the rest of the ministry continues to move forward. You're able to accomplish more, and others experience the blessing of serving. In addition, your team members' skills are sharpened for other works God has planned for them in the future.

The coolest benefit of delegation is watching others become so passionate and involved in the Church that they hear a clear call on their lives to be in ministry. This has happened with kids who grew up in my children's ministry. It has happened with adult leaders who left their jobs to go into full or part-time ministry. I've also seen key volunteer leaders step up and take over when God called me to another place. Good delegation creates an awesome legacy, and it's a testament to the work God has done through you.

As I wrote this chapter, I thought about a man who stepped up to lead a ministry I left quite a few years ago. Mr. Mickey was the obvious choice to guide that children's ministry through many transitions after I left. With the help of a solid team, he kept the ministry going as the church itself struggled through a lot of change. He was another man who knew the importance of delegation. I was blessed to have him on my lead ministry team for seven years, a team that graciously stuck with me as I learned how to delegate effectively. When I left, Mr. Mickey took over, and he became the one pouring into the team, investing in them, and equipping them to minister.

When Mr. Mickey was diagnosed with cancer, the children's ministry kept moving forward. Throughout his difficult battle, Mr. Mickey repeated his personal mantra, "God wins!" He proclaimed that whether God healed his body or called him home, God still won. This applied to his ministry as well. Whether he was there or not, it would keep going because he delegated and equipped the volunteers well. Mr. Mickey made his ministry stronger with delegation; he truly set it up to win!

My friend and co-laborer went home to the Lord in February 2019. Mr. Mickey left an amazing legacy that continues to point children and adults to the love and saving grace of Jesus. Please understand that your ministry is so much bigger than you alone. Create your own legacy by sharing the work and blessings of ministry through effective delegation. You and your children's ministry will be stronger when you do!

Pastor Butch is a 20-year veteran as an innovative and creative children's pastor who loves combing through kids' movies to find excellent leadership principles. He's also a devoted husband to one, a loving dad to 4 adult children, and an incredible Popz to 4 little tykes.

chapter 14

PUT A LITTLE SEASONING ON IT

*You are stronger when you
learn from those who came before.*

BY AARON LABARGE

ANYTIME SOMEONE SAYS, "It tastes like chicken," I know I'm going to hear "That's because chicken supposedly has no flavor, and it tastes like whatever you season it with." What's crazy about that statement is how it is true in other situations. When it comes to ministry, you're seasoned by those before you. So, your ministry will have a similar style or "taste" like that prior influence. For example, if someone asked you why you do ministry the way you do it, you will point to a book or directly to a person you learned it from. When teaching kids, I've been known to stand on furniture or throw something up in the air at random. I do this because I had a science teacher who did it when I was young. To this day, I can remember a book flying across the room to teach us about gravity. He seasoned the ministry God called me to. Taking what I learned from someone who has been teaching a lot longer than me has impacted my ministry. That's what is so great about learning from seasoned kidmin leaders. When allowed, these seasoned people can add excellent flavor to the ministry you're doing.

PUT IT IN THE OVEN

For anyone who has ever said or been told, "Dinner's ready. You just have to put it in the oven" should see the significance of help. If you're the one being told this, someone in the house is a better cook than you. In my case, it's my wife reaching out the olive branch of help, because she definitely knows cooking isn't my specialty. I find it extremely helpful when she does this for me, because it's like I'm starting ahead of the game. She's a great cook and has a better understanding of it than I do, so she already knows what seasonings will work with certain foods. This is what it's like when you learn from leaders who have paved the way. They know what works, because they've done it before. They know what it's going to take to get little Tommy's attention, because they've taught a bunch of little "Tommys."

SUGAR IN THE CHILI

Speaking of my wife's awesome cooking, one day I saw her put sugar in chili. My first thought was sugar is sweet and chili isn't, so that didn't make any logical since. Then my wife explained to me that the sugar offsets the acidity of the tomatoes, which made sense. In my mind, sugar shouldn't go in chili, but she knew better because she had studied it, she had read about it, she had learned from others, but even more importantly, she had done it! She had a greater base of knowledge because her passion for cooking led her to learn these things. What's so awesome, though, about learning that from my wife is that I didn't have to do any of the hard work she did to get that information. I know now that sugar can go in chili and I know why. Because of my wife, I got to skip ahead and not spend all the time and energy she put in. Some would say maybe I cheated the system, but that's not it at all. She was happy to teach me what she knew, because she knew it would make me better at making chili. And she was right. Since then, I've made some pretty good chili with my new secret ingredient—sugar.

SPICE GIRL

Geri Halliwell, one member of the music group, The Spice Girls, once said, "Someone taught me how to eat properly. Learning from others is important when it's not working for yourself." The issue most people have is that they always think they know better than someone else. What Geri was saying is that everyone has to be taught how to eat by people who already know how to eat. There's little to no difference between this and how you learn about ministry. Senior kidmin leaders have walked the walk and they have talked the talk, so let them teach you what they know. At the very least, it will put you ahead of the game.

OOOH, THE BIBLE

When trying to understanding virtually anything as a Christian, you should always look toward Scripture. When it comes to learning from others, especially those who have been at it longer, Scripture has so many references of this happening. You might say it is sprinkled in (just to keep the cooking theme alive). The first two people most people think of is Paul and Barnabas. These two men were mentoring everyone they could. Paul especially took his time to help Timothy. Timothy was a younger minister and all through his and Paul's encounters, Paul encouraged and taught Timothy. In 1 Timothy 4:12, Paul tells Timothy, *"Let no one look down on your youthfulness, but rather in speech, conduct, love, faith and purity, show yourself an example of those who believe"* (NASB). One can only imagine how special those words were to Timothy, because Paul knew the struggle Timothy was going through. In Paul's early ministry, people gave him a lot of grief for his prior life. Paul knew it was hard to stay focused when the world seemed to be coming down on you. He took that knowledge and lifted Timothy up. But what does this mean for you? Timothy had a choice in the matter. He could have ignored the wise words of Paul and decided that he could figure it out on his own. He could have told Paul, "You just don't get it. Times are changing." Rather, he listened and he grew. You can grow, also. You just have to stop and listen.

TWO-DOLLAR WORD OF THE DAY IS CHRONOCENTRISM

Today, many people see themselves as the pentacle of greatness. "We are the most intelligent people to ever live," they might say. This thought leads people to look down on or ignore those who came before them. This is known as chronocentrism, which is a word coined by sociologist Jib Fowles. He presented the concept in a journal called *Futures*. He defined it as "the belief that one's own times are paramount, that other periods pale in comparison." The point of bringing this word to your attention is that this happens in ministry all the time. People say things like, "They just don't understand" or "Things are different today." What if Timothy had told Paul that? He may have still done great ministry, but would it have been his best ministry?

What should be noted is that even though some things do change, a lot of things stay the same. Most importantly, God doesn't change, so the ideas of those before you should empower you because they served the same unchanged God that you are. Although technology changes, that doesn't mean that God changes. Ultimately, those who walked before you were just trying to teach kids about God in the best way they could. You can learn from the mere fact they have taught kids, and discover more lessons on who Christ is. They get it! They may not understand how to use Facebook, but they understand kids and how God loves kids.

ORANGE JUICE IN CEREAL?

With every great idea there are a lot of bad ones. If you've seen gross food combination videos or articles, one that keeps appearing is where people replace milk in their cereal with orange juice. I'm sorry, but that is disgusting. Yes, orange juice is definitely a breakfast item, but it's not going on my cereal! Just because something seems like it should work or, as they say, "It looks good on paper," doesn't mean it actually will work.

The same goes for when you're seeking to learn from leaders. Some people are awesome Christians who love Jesus, but they may not be the best person from which you can learn. You need to seek out people who are going to build your ministry. Seek out leaders who understand what God has called you to accomplish. That doesn't mean ignore everyone else, but it does mean that you should be intentional. You can get lost trying to read every single thing out there about "how to run your children's ministry." So, seek out leaders who are going to grow you and your ministry. Don't get lost in the big idea of today. Instead, focus on where God has you. Don't be fooled into thinking you need orange juice in your cereal because everyone else is doing it. Instead, stay the course, as Paul told Timothy, and seek out those who will encourage and help you do so.

NOT JUST WORDS

These are not just meaningless words for me. When stepping into ministry, there were a lot of unknowns for me, as you probably experienced yourself. The greatest keys to my success in ministry are nothing that I've done; instead, they are the work of God and others who poured into me. Starting out in ministry is scary. To be able to listen to and be encouraged by people like Tina Houser when I first started was huge.

Outwardly, Tina and I seem like polar opposites, but when it comes to teaching, our styles match perfectly. So, when looking for ways to do something different, she was someone I gleaned from... not to sell people like Ryan Frank or Brian Dollar short, because I also learned a lot from them. If you ever get the chance, ask Brian Dollar to tell you about the plagues of Egypt. Brian will teach you that not every idea you have is going to work, but that doesn't mean you stop trying. It also doesn't mean you give up on having new ideas. These are not the only people who can encourage and teach you. There are people in your area who have been teaching kids a long time, like a retired teacher who might be a member of your church. Don't be scared to seek them out and learn from them. Be encouraged by them. Don't ignore them just because "the world is changing." Take what they have learned and carry it further.

GREAT-GRANDMA'S RECIPE

A lot of families have a special recipe that is passed down from generation to generation. When you learn from other leaders, it's like you become the keeper of Great-Grandma's recipe. You get to ensure that everyone in the future benefits from its awesomeness. The leaders who came before you are not trying to hold you back. They're trying to lift you up by passing on what they have, so you can take it to the next level. You can also use that recipe and share it with the next generation. The leaders who have lived their time and done their work understand Paul's words in 2 Timothy 4:6-8, when he said, *"For I am already being poured out as a drink offering, and the time of my departure has come. I have fought the good fight, I have finished the course, I have kept the faith; in the future there is laid up a crown of righteousness, which the Lord, the righteous Judge, will award to me on that day; and not only to me, but also to all who have loved His appearing"* (NASB). They know that one day it will be your time and you will be the one fighting the good fight. They want you to be ready. So please just listen, grow, and learn.

Aaron LaBarge currently serves as the Family Pastor at a church in Columbia, KY. He is a father of 4 and is married to the lovely Jenny LaBarge. Before going into ministry full time, he was in the U.S. Army for 8 years. Outside of the church, he also runs a family blog, labargefamilyministry.com and is the co-host of a podcast called Childish Behavior, built to encourage those in family, youth, and children's ministry. His passion is to teach and mold children and their families to grow in Christ together, by empowering family-based teaching as the cornerstone of faith learning.

chapter 15

BETTER TOGETHER!

You are stronger when you have a network of support.

BY LORI GRASTY

D O YOU FEEL LIKE you're pushing the same rock up the same hill? *Every. Week.* Maybe it's the same challenges but a new week or new month? Do these challenges perhaps include not having enough volunteers to fill the schedule, a fear of looking at your phone or email for inevitable cancellations, curriculum that does a lackluster job of explaining key biblical concepts—or it requires abundant resources, preparation, and supplies that you just don't have. I get it. We get it.

Your church uniquely ministers to children in a vast variety of ways and contexts—location, size, and structure. Yet, many times the challenges are very similar. Culture is changing, expectations are changing, and church habits are changing. But we are in it together, facing the same obstacles and the same challenges. Your frustrations are often very similar though in very different locations and environments. As children's ministers, or children's pastors, or kidmin directors—or whatever your names may be—you know a lot about your field. You know children, trends, ministry, scripture, classroom management, discipline, volunteer recruitment... but do you know each other?

I often hear statements about how isolating it can feel to be in children's ministry. While you love being with kids, you often miss out on the conversations that the larger church may be having or you tend to have a different perspective coming from your experience with children. It can be discouraging and maybe lonely too, but I've found that connecting with other individuals in children's ministry is a vital source of support and encouragement.

SMALL START: SOCIAL MEDIA

So maybe you're feeling alone in what you do... perhaps a bit underwhelmed or uninspired? A great starting point for both resources and connection are social media sites. Consider following leaders in the field and those you admire. These individuals (or groups) often offer great ideas, a new perspective, and sources of inspiration. Joining a Facebook group is a key opportunity for connection. There are a lot of great conversations taking place in groups which are closed (private) and allow for troubleshooting, brainstorming, encouragement, and venting!

The advantage to a social media connection is that you can do it at your convenience. It does not require time away from the office or travel, which makes it an easy resource. Consider thinking of it as a conversation too. While you can rely on it for resources, you're also able to engage, listen, and support the challenges others are having. Oftentimes, it serves to remind you of how far you've come in a given area. It helps you appreciate challenges you don't (currently) face, and may offer a new (national or global) perspective that you might not have been afforded in your local community.

Social media connections do, however, lack personal connection, unless you're extremely intentional or connect individually with someone specifically. Therefore, most times, they serve as a good resource but are a bit impersonal. So, think of it as maybe a first step, but not your only source of community and connection in the field.

BETTER YET: COMMUNITY CONNECTION

Do you have a local network in your community that provides you a source of support? I'm grateful that our area has a children's ministry connection group that meets quarterly throughout the year. It's a place for those in similar roles at different churches and in various denominations or non-denominations to gather.

Unfortunately, sometimes children's ministry directors view the kidmin at other churches as the competition. However, there's plenty of competition in the world outside of the church without adding your co-workers in ministry to the list. You're on the same team. Larger threats to your mission come in the form of limited time, changing priorities, youth sports on Sundays, negative church experiences, and many others, as you know.

If the goal is to make disciples or bring kids to Jesus (insert your own mission statement here), you *can* and *should* work together to share ideas and collaborate. Partnerships and communication help to prevent you from running the same VBS program during the same week of the summer as other area churches. Perhaps you've come to the realization that you are the 100th church in your local area running a Trunk-N-Treat event or an Easter Egg Hunt. It might be time to consider if it's really worth it. Local area and wider area connection opportunities allow for the chance to work together and communicate with one another so that you can all work smarter and not harder.

For me this realization came with a Trunk-N-Treat event. We offered this experience for many years but other churches started to do so also and they did it really well (festivals, lots of cars, inside games, community partnerships). Our leadership team evaluated if this event was still in line with our mission and if it was an effective and fruitful use of ministry resources. We decided that it was not. While it provided a lot of candy for children, we consistently struggled to get enough cars to participate. Letting go of this event allowed us to more intentionally focus on other areas we could do more successfully that built on our current schedule.

Instead, we chose to offer a family evening Christmas experience that could take place during our regularly scheduled Wednesday night programming. It required less additional volunteers and allowed us to connect with a group of families whose children were currently engaged. It helped us build relationships with the families of our children, as well as our larger church community was grateful for an event that offered them a chance to invite their friends and family. It further provided a platform to introduce or expand on the Christmas story for children and equip parents/families with a faith language for this important time of year that often trends toward commercial influence. It was a win/win for us, our current families, and our local/neighborhood community. And some of our parents celebrated that their children had less Halloween candy, too!

I'll be honest, it took me a few years to come to this conclusion happily. It didn't happen overnight. We licked our wounds and complained about everyone else doing Halloween events and not having enough volunteers to do ours. We eventually realized that many of the groups taking up this cause were not churches, but community organizations and schools. I was able to realize that we were not offering a unique, safe experience for our community to have a faith-based exposure during a secular holiday. Instead, we really were just handing out a lot of candy. Now, we can celebrate, support, and attend the community organizations and other churches that are doing Halloween events better than we were. *Side note:* A great way to support these organizations is to share their events on your social media sites and ask them for permission to list their activities on your calendar, if it is something you feel comfortable recommending. Most often, this is a good start to building partnerships and collaboration!

Keeping in mind that our competition is not other churches (and it is likely not community groups that are working towards equipping children) helps you align your priorities and support one another. The needs and challenges children and families face are plenty. Partnership ministries are often more effective than duplicate ministries. Creating opportunities for conversation allows you to work together and offers a chance for these partnerships to flourish.

So, if you do not have a local area group that meets regularly, maybe consider inviting a few individuals from other churches in your area to a brown bag lunch session to talk about one or two key ideas? It does not have to be anything elaborate. Sometimes big goals face a lot of obstacles before they're actually implemented. However, if you start with the goal of inviting a few churches, it can be a chance for others to get out of the office and see other children ministry spaces. Think of it as an opportunity to talk with experts in the field and share celebrations, as well as address current challenges. You never know what kind of ideas and opportunities might come out of this time together!

BEST CASE: FIND A BESTIE!

Through my church's denominational camping ministry, I happened upon (and was greatly blessed with) a church partnership. Our church had been going to a church camp for years at the same time as a few other local area churches from our denomination. After a few years of observation, I made the decision to join the leadership team for one week of summer camp. This provided a great opportunity for me (and eventually our team) to partner with another church's children's ministry team. We started with a summer camp partnership and have grown to do year-round ministry together.

In planning for summer camp, we designated a time once a month to spend the entire day dreaming and planning for camp. We implemented curriculum, planned messages, came up with crazy activities and games. Then we went during the summer for a week of camp and pulled the whole thing to life leading children on the journey... together.

Let me tell you, there is not much better (for me, at least) than to feel like I'm part of a team doing children's ministry toward a common goal and with a shared knowledge. There are plenty of times when I have planned a great game that completely flopped and I found myself with a lot of time to pass. Or there are other times when I've had a child who pushed my buttons and brought me to the point of wondering, "Okay, what next?" To have someone walk that path with me was encouraging, refreshing, and inspiring. In fact, we both felt this rejuvenation and realized we needed it.

After a collective 40+ years in faith-based programs and children's ministry, we needed someone who could finish our sentences when our words ran out and someone who could give our ideas the extra sparkle, glitter, or dose of slime to make them amazing. This teamwork offered the presence of someone who could be the extra set of eyes for supervision, and who knew the beginning, middle, and end of all parts of the confidential conversations that normally only the director is privilege too. Once we realized how much better it made us individually to do ministry together, we have since added a winter retreat we go on, in addition to a summer experience. A unique result that came from this relationship is that our friendship created a special synergy for both of us, as well as it also created relationships between our kids at two different churches. Not only do we want to do camp and retreats together because it feeds our souls, but our kids are champions of the idea as well. They look forward to an opportunity to do something with their friends from the other church that have become part of their faith journeys. What a unique experience that celebrates the community of the church in a tangible way for kids!

After three years, we have committed to meeting once a month for a long breakfast or lunch. At these meetings, we talk about challenges we're facing, solutions that have worked for us, and areas of frustration (no holds barred conversations where you can vent with your whole heart and completely move on after you get it all out). We talk about our daily schedules, goals, areas of supervision, challenging kids, incentive/behavior programs, holiday events, parenting with parents, books we've read, trainings we've been to, new kidmin songs, curriculum, finding inspiration, hiring, letting staff go, framing conversations, being creative... you get the point.

It took us a while to find the time, and some months it's much harder than others. The demands of children's ministry are never ending and getting away is not easy. But it has become a priority for both of us because we are better in individual careers due to our support and encouragement for one another... so we make it happen. And if we didn't, there's a chance that one or both of us might not still be in children's ministry!

This is a unique situation that cannot be replicated. God works in really unique and encouraging ways so you never know what might be out there for you until you try. It's worth the effort. Friendships and collaboration are an important part of doing children's ministry, so try to reach out to new children's ministry directors and invite them to lunch. If money is an obstacle, perhaps bring a lunch and eat it together in a common space at your church. But it's important that you look out for one another and encourage each other on the journey. It is these relationships that make you stronger personally and in ministry.

Lori Grasty is a licensed local pastor in the United Methodist Church and serves as the Director of Children and Family Ministry at Trinity on Jackson in northern Indiana. Her favorite quote was provided by a child tasked with writing a card of encouragement which said on the front "Jesus loves you" and on the inside "so suck it up!"

chapter 16

A MENTOR'S MARK

You are stronger when you have a mentor.

BY JARED LILLY

IN A SENSE, I find myself to be the most and least qualified person to be contributing to a project such as this, and I'll explain why in a moment. I have been involved in kidmin since I was a teen. I was raised in church by my mother and my grandparents on both sides of my family. My father, however, was never one to cling to the church or its beliefs and traditions. Retrospectively, I can see that I was looking for a Christian male influence who could show me what it meant to be a "man of God", so to speak. I found him, and he was my children's pastor, Pastor Greg. As great as my dad was, this man stood in the gap spiritually in places where my father never did. It was only a matter of time before I found myself wanting to be a children's pastor.

I remember coming home from camp the year I felt like the Lord had called me to children's ministry. I did everything I could to learn more and be involved. I even found out which school bus stopped closest to my church so I could walk to the church and follow Greg around all day. (Who knows how many hours I set him back in his day-to-day.) Most people, myself included, would have sought out a way to tell 13-year-old me to chill out. Pastor Greg never did. He listened to me, pointed me to Jesus, affirmed the call of God on my life, and equipped me to respond to that call.

This is why I say I'm the most and least qualified person to be writing to you now: I have yet to even finish a bachelor's degree, but due to God's faithfulness to me and to those He's placed in my life, I've had the opportunity to serve God full-time in ministry my entire adult life.

There are countless examples of mentoring relationships throughout scripture: Elijah and Elisha, Paul and Timothy, Jesus and the Disciples. My favorite snapshot of biblical mentoring, though, has to come from 1 Samuel 3, which chronicles Samuel's call from God. As you examine 1 Samuel 3, you can identify at least five things a mentor can bring to the life of a kidmin leader.

COVERING

"The boy Samuel served the Lord in Eli's presence. In those days the word of the Lord was rare and prophetic visions were not widespread" (1 Samuel 3:1 CSB).

One thing I love about this stage of Samuel's life is that he isn't a prophet yet! Like the Lord, an effective mentor will take you from your starting point, no matter where it is. They are your covering! While I served under Pastor Greg, I tried some stupid stuff, like the object lesson where I sent people into the attic so they could throw down boxes full of "gifts from above" onto the stage I was standing on... and it was okay. I avoided a concussion, the adults had a good laugh, and the lesson was memorable. Afterwards, Greg and I had a discussion on what went well and what I should never ever do again. (Insider tip: It was the box thing. I probably could've gotten away with throwing empty boxes.) It wasn't just one conversation on that one day. We had countless conversations—after great days, after bad days, and on days where I just felt like I needed to talk. I had the space to make mistakes and discoveries and to find my voice.

A mentor providing this kind of supervision is foundational, but it will only take you so far. There comes a point in your relationship with your mentor when you're no longer being supervised by them and the dynamic of the relationship shifts. Rather than being supervised, you call them ahead of decisions, events, and campaigns. You're able to do this because a mentor's covering is beyond supervision. A mentor covers you in prayer, love, friendship, and affirmation. Even if you no longer *"serve in Eli's presence"*, having that sort of covering unlocks a strength and a freedom that will carry you for years!

CONSISTENTLY ACCESSIBLE

"One day Eli, whose eyesight was failing, was lying in his usual place..." (1 Samuel 3:2, CSB).

Hopefully by this point, you've decided to read through 1 Samuel 3 yourself. If not, it's okay; I'll help you out. In the verses that follow, Samuel hears God call out to him. He doesn't recognize God's voice, because he's never heard it before, so he mistakes it to be Eli.

Samuel knows exactly where to find Eli, because he was lying where he always laid. Samuel didn't have to go looking for Eli. Otherwise, he may have assumed he was hearing things and gone back to bed. Effective mentors are consistent. They don't just show up to criticize you when you've messed up and they don't claim you when you've done something great. They are consistently in your corner, cheering for you, offering a shoulder to cry on, or a sounding board to let you know whether or not you're crazy! You don't have to look for them. My mentors were there for me when my parents divorced, when my loved ones died, when I graduated high school, when I got engaged, when I got married, and when my wife gave birth to our kids. I didn't find them *"lying in their usual place"* literally, but they took my call or called me. I didn't have to search them out. You are blessed in that your "usual place" for connecting with your mentors is usually found in the phone you carry in your pocket! That's one of the great things about being in the kidmin community at this point in history: technology allows for more consistent communication. At any given moment you can log on to a multitude of websites and social media platforms to connect and glean from the wisdom of thousands of other kidmin leaders!

IDENTIFY THE VOICE OF GOD

"Now Samuel did not yet know the Lord, because the word of the Lord had not yet been revealed to him... Then Eli understood that the Lord was calling the boy" (1 Samuel 3:7,8b CSB).

You know the feeling of having 100 different voices calling for your attention. Sometimes it's a boss or a pastor giving correction, or it's your family calling for much needed attention after a busy season of ministry has stolen your focus. There are times when you're bombarded with well-intentioned people giving advice for what they would do in your situation and there are times when Satan intentionally puts voices in your life to deceive you. With all these voices constantly ringing in your ears, it can be difficult to discern the voice of God in your life! Trusted mentors make you stronger by identifying that voice in your life. When you try your hardest and can't make any headway, a mentor will step in and tell you that God is telling you to rest. When you feel restless and discontent, a mentor can walk you through whether the Lord would have you refocus or look towards transition. Often times, a mentor can help you realize the Lord is calling you to something greater when you didn't recognize it yourself, as is the case for Samuel. They are the ones who constantly point you to Christ by saying, "Have you prayed about it?", "What do you think the Lord might be speaking to you?", or sometimes even "God is telling you to (insert your calling here)!"

Although you are constantly inundated with voices clamoring for attention, you know from Elijah that often times God is not found in the storms or in the earthquakes, but in the whisper. Without allowing a mentor into your life, you run the risk of dismissing that whisper as other issues compete for your time, your energy, and your focus. How wonderful it is that God in His infinite wisdom created you to be in relationship with one another so that your mentors can point you right back to Him.

TEACH US HOW TO RESPOND

"He told Samuel, "Go and lie down, if he calls you say, 'Speak, Lord, for your servant is listening.' So, Samuel went and lay down in his place" (1 Samuel 3:9, CSB).

As powerful as it is to have a mentor in your life who can point out the voice of God, it does no good to recognize the Lord if you don't know how to respond to Him. Just as Eli told Samuel to respond, a mentor will not only acknowledge the voice of God, but will give you practical steps in how to respond to the Lord. This is one of the most incredible impacts a mentor can have in your life, because the insight you receive from a mentor on any given topic is often built on and used throughout your life. Take a look at Samuel. Because Eli taught him to recognize and respond to the Lord, he goes on to anoint the first two kings of Israel—Saul and David—and is known as a prophet throughout the land. What would have become of one of the most influential prophets in Israel's history had he not had a mentor in Eli? When your mentors speak into your life, you are strengthened both in the present and eternally, as they have given you practicality for today and wisdom for tomorrow. Nearly every decision I've made in ministry is built on a foundation of knowledge handed to me by the trusted mentors in my life.

OPENNESS AND AFFIRMATION

"Samuel lay down until the morning; then he opened the doors of the Lord's house. He was afraid to tell Eli the vision, but Eli called him and said, 'Samuel, my son.' 'Here I am,' answered Samuel. 'What was the message he gave you?' Eli asked. 'Don't hide it from me. May God punish you and do so severely if you hide anything from me that he told you'" (1 Samuel 3:15-17, CSB).

The success of a mentoring relationship is corollary to how open you are willing to be with your mentor. Eli doesn't merely ask Samuel how things are going; he demands openness. This is vital. If you desire to maximize your capacity for growth, you need to be willing to put it all out there with your mentor. Samuel was understandably afraid to share what the Lord had spoken to him, as it was grave news for Eli. Having been raised in the Lord's house, he was more than likely aware of the stories in the Old Testament—stories of a prophet delivering bad news and then being killed for it! Imagine if you heard the voice of God for the first time and the message was that *"the iniquity of Eli's family will never be wiped out by either sacrifice or offering"* (1 Samuel 3:14, CSB)? I certainly wouldn't want to be the one to deliver that message to Eli! Think about all the things you've ever held in your heart, wondering if it was something God had given you or not. How many times have you kept those things hidden because you were afraid of what someone may think?

During a prayer meeting years ago, I thought I heard the Lord tell me that a woman on our volunteer team was going to be expecting. I knew this woman and her husband had been struggling with fertility. In fact, she had recently stepped away as this desire caused her to occasionally weep over the infants in her care. I was terrified to share this with her. If I was hearing the Lord correctly, this was great news! However, if I was caught up in the emotion of the evening and was wrong, I could deliver this woman with a false hope. I was fortunate that my mentors had not only helped me identify the voice of God, but affirmed it when I shared that I heard it! I told the woman what was on my heart and she gave birth 10 months later!

Sometimes, you allow fear to discourage you from pursuing and sharing what the Lord is doing in your life. Because I had mentors who affirmed the voice of God in my life, I was able to find confidence in what the Lord was speaking to me. This is what Eli does for Samuel when he says *"He is the Lord. Let him do what he thinks is good"* (1 Samuel 3:18b, CSB) after hearing the bad news. This is what your mentors will do for you, too. Once they've helped you recognize the voice of God, they affirm the things He says! They give you the space to share the things that are crazy, the things that are hard to decipher, and the things that scare you, and will affirm those things that God has said. Their ability to do so is predicated on your willingness to be open with them and not hold back, even when it scares you.

BE INTENTIONAL

I don't care if you serve in your church's 10-kid VBS every summer or if you are the children's pastor of a megachurch, you need mentors in your life. For some, this simply means looking around and seeing who God has placed in your life. Samuel didn't have much of a choice; Eli raised him! For others, this means seeking out and asking someone to allow you to follow them. This was common in the rabbinic tradition. For some, the mentor may seek you out and beckon you to "follow me" as Christ did for His disciples. Regardless of which of these categories you fall into, success will be found in your intentionality. Don't hesitate to tell someone in your life that you admire them and want them to mentor you. It's a high honor for them and, should they agree, it will pay dividends for you in your life and ministry. Schedule times to speak with them regularly and often.

Finally, an effective mentor produces mentors. 1 Samuel 19:20 describes, *"... they saw the group of prophets prophesying with Samuel leading them ..."* (CSB). As you grow and maintain your relationship with your mentor, be sure to find a Samuel of your own!

Jared Lilly is a husband to Hannah, father to McKenna and Abby, and the children's pastor at First Assembly in Gastonia, NC. When not serving in church ministry he loves to spend time with his family, watch football, and play music.

chapter 17

DANCING ON UNKNOWN STAGES

You are stronger when you have friends—
both saved and unsaved.

BY NINA DURNING

FLING. SEANN TRIUBHAS. Strathspey. Jig. Piobaireachd. No, I didn't just run my fingers across the computer keyboard. Unless you have an understanding of Scottish arts, culture, and tradition, these words may seem strange or even foreign to you. A fling and seann triubhas are two Scottish highland dances, and a strathspey, jig, and piobaireachd are three different genres of bagpipe music. My husband and I have unique hobbies rooted in Scottish tradition; my husband is a bagpiper and I am a highland dancer. When we first met, my husband had been playing the great highland bagpipe for ten years and had been competing for about nine. While I was intrigued by this talent, what fascinated me even more were the thousands of people who gathered together for events surrounding this culture. My first experience with it was in 2011 at the Highland Games in New Hampshire. Thousands of people came dressed to perfection in clan tartans, kilts, and ghillies (shoes) to spectate all the wonderful Scottish traditions. There were pipe bands, solo pipers, dancers, fiddlers, strong men in athletics, and so much great food. I was in awe... and in shock that I never knew such a community of people existed so close to my home!

I walked around, following my husband's shadow from event to event, and was introduced to so many people he had befriended over the years. The more events I went to after that first experience, the more I found myself surrounded by a crowd that was very different from myself. They spoke in language that I would not recommend, they behaved in manners I considered inappropriate, and it made me uncomfortable. It made me uneasy. That's when I realized, I lived in a Christian "bubble" that I had created. It shouldn't have surprised me that unbelievers would do and say the things they did. Yet, here I was, surprised and uncomfortable.

Since I work in predominantly Christian settings, I found that my compassion for the lost wasn't growing or being challenged. I didn't feel an urgency to share the Gospel, often allowing opportunities to slip by. I was comfortable where I was, with my Christian friends, my church, and inner circle. God needed to strategically place me in a community where I could be challenged to love those who do not love Him. Being surrounded by unbelievers more has reminded me that God has called the believer to be in community with those who have not yet received Christ. When surrounded by the Christian community regularly, believers can find themselves only in Christian environments. It's not that they intend to have no unsaved friends, but so often the by-product is just that. God has called His people to have compassion for those who are lost. *"Let your light shine before others, that they may see your good deeds and glorify your Father in heaven"* (Matthew 5:16, NIV). God desires that your life be a testimony to who He is and how He can impact the life of the one watching you. When your life is put on display, it allows the unbeliever to see how good God is and what He can do in their own life. I needed to be challenged in that way. I needed to become someone who could boldly give hope to the hopeless, but I had to find myself in a circle of people who needed hope.

So, I committed to dancing on an unknown stage, literally. I endeavored to be truly a part of the community in which God had strategically placed my husband and me. I started taking highland dance lessons, and even began competing. As I became more involved, getting to know more people, my heart began to see them in the way God saw them. I noticed the loneliness some faced. I saw the bondage of alcoholism and addiction in others. I saw the desire for something more in those who had questions that seemed to have no answers. God placed within me a heart of compassion for lost people. As I interacted with unbelievers at the events and classes, I saw their desperate need for a Savior and my heart broke for them. I've now been dancing for three years and have built relationships where I'm bold when I talk about my church and my faith. I say, "I'll be praying for you" and they know I mean it. As I dance alongside them, am taught by them, and show my interest in their lives, my desire is that I would be able to share the message of Jesus with them. I want Him to be glorified as some of the unbelievers in my life become believers.

This desire does not come without its challenges, however. In a community where God can seem to be very absent, my husband and I planted ourselves and believed that God would impact people through us despite opposition. But the opposition was very real and at times difficult. Some made snickering jokes when we ordered soda water instead of a beer. Others brought up religion or social issues just to provoke arguments or challenging conversation. At first, these interactions made me feel so uncomfortable. I shied away from the conversation, or found an excuse to leave for a few minutes, leaving my husband to fend for himself. I felt as though my faith, the foundation I had built my entire life on, was under attack and I wasn't confident in defending it. While it was hard, I had to remember that *"everyone who wants to live a godly life in Christ Jesus will be persecuted"* (2 Timothy 3:12, NIV). I knew that God put us in this environment not for our own comfort, but rather because the people around us needed Jesus and we were their connection to Him. I had to learn how to answer the tough questions and defend my faith beliefs; as a result, it made me a stronger believer. I practiced answering difficult theological questions, rehearsing my answers and rebuttals to follow up arguments. I dug deeper into my own faith and beliefs, really questioning myself on why I believed the Gospel and the Bible to be true. This not only made me a stronger apologetic, but it made me a stronger Christian. I was confident in what I believed, no doubts or disbelief. I knew what Jesus had done for me, and I could defend the Scriptures that taught us His story.

"He must hold firmly to the trustworthy message as it has been taught, so that he can encourage others by sound doctrine and refute those who oppose it" (Titus 1:9, NIV). Challenging your own beliefs is not a bad thing. It firms within your heart the truth of God's Word. It gives you the doctrine and teachings that help reveal sin in the unbeliever's life so they can see it. This revealing must be done in truth, but also in love. *"Be wise in the way you act toward outsiders; make the most of every opportunity. Let your conversation be always full of grace, seasoned with salt, so that you may know how to answer everyone"* (Colossians 4:5-6, NIV).

When the challenges come from the unbeliever, it's important that you speak in grace and with wise words. As God walks with you, through those opportunities, pause and allow the

Spirit to grant you the words to say. When you've put in the time to study, testing your own beliefs, you will be able to give a sound defense. So, who is in your life who does not know God? Who in your life challenges your faith? Who in your life are you witnessing to?

My husband's best friend, another piper, is the person in our lives who God has given us to love on and witness to. He enjoys having theological conversations about faith. He is an unbeliever, yet reads the Bible more than most Christians I know, and he has lots of questions about Christian practices. My husband spends hours talking with his friend about faith, answering question after question, giving sound arguments in defense of Christ. We have spent time defending prayer, creation, Jesus' humanity and deity, among other things. Our friend will push back, and we will answer. Time and time again, we have prayed that God would reveal Himself. While we have not seen our friend come to faith yet, we believe that the seeds we are planting, even despite his opposition, will reap a harvest one day.

Befriending the unbeliever is like dancing on an unknown stage. It's scary because it's new and uncertain. You might not know your audience that is watching, and you may have a terrible fear of being judged by them. However, God has called you to be in the world, standing firm for your faith as a light to all who do not know Him. *"For I am not ashamed of the gospel, for it is the power of God for salvation to everyone who believes, to the Jew first and also to the Greek"* (Romans 1:16, NIV). You are stronger when you develop a compassion for the lost and can see people through God's eyes. You are stronger when you learn to defend your faith, speaking both grace and truth to bring life into those who do not know God.

While you dance on stages that are unknown, you also need to remember the importance of dancing on stages that you do know within your faith community. The faith community is designed to strengthen, encourage, and keep you accountable in your faith.

"Two are better than one, because they have a good return for their labor: If either of them falls down, one can help the other up. But pity anyone who falls and has no one to help them up. Also, if two lie down together, they will keep warm. But how can one keep warm alone? Though one may be overpowered, two can defend themselves. A cord of three strands is not quickly broken" (Ecclesiastes 4:9-12, NIV).

Having close friends in the faith community provides a strength in times of weakness or doubt. When I was challenging my own beliefs and being challenged by others, having strong Christian friends around me helped me get back up when I felt as though my faith had been knocked down. Sometimes it was a scripture that they brought back to my memory, or just a prayer of support that helped me get back to a strong place of faith.

My Christian circle of friends helped me stay encouraged in difficult times of ministry or life. Life is going to throw you things that are unexpected and you really shouldn't be surprised by it. This world is fallen, sinful, and therefore negative things are going to happen. How you respond to those moments is what identifies your faith or lack thereof. When you have a close faith-filled friend who can come alongside you in moments of trial, it helps your response to be one of faith, trusting God to come through in ways that only He can. I have a best friend, who I've known for 20 years. We grew up together in my father's church and we became inseparable by the time we were ten. We both serve in ministry full-time and when either of us has a moment, or a trial, or anything, we immediately contact the other for support. Why? Because *"two are better than one."* She is the one I know will storm heaven for me and vice versa. We find strength and encouragement in one another when the difficult times come. Together we seek God and His faithfulness.

Close Christian friends also provide accountability that's necessary for spiritual growth. Every person needs to have one other they can confide in and be comfortable with sharing their faults with. *"Listen to advice and accept discipline, and at the end, you will be counted among the wise"* (Proverbs 19:20, NIV). You need to have a partner who will be able to point out your flaws and who will hold you to a higher standard of morality. The world can lead you astray and tempt you with things that might seem harmless, but are not good for your spirit. The Lord has called you to *"not conform to the pattern of this world, but be transformed by the renewing of your mind"* (Romans 12:2, NIV). In order to live that out, you must have someone else in your life who will help you maintain your boundaries and a standard of righteousness that God desires. Who in your life serves as that accountability? What in your life do you know you need someone else's support in overcoming? What step can you make today to find that person for your life?

As you dance on unknown stages, seeking lost people for the kingdom of God, know that God desires your heart to be compassionate. He wants you to trust in His Word as your foundation. He wants you to love people because He loves them. Be bold in your faith, be challenged by the unbeliever, and be stronger as you learn to defend the Gospel of Jesus. Also, be wise in choosing friends. Have close Christian support around you that will be a source of strength, encouragement, and accountability. Let them be your encouragement as you witness to those in your life who do not know Christ. Let them keep you on the straight path when temptations from the unknown stage come your way. Allow them to strengthen your faith.

Nina Durning served as the Children's Pastor of Calvary Christian Church in Lynnfield, MA for five years. She is a competitive highland dancer, loves to cook, and loves her husband Bobby who plays bagpipes.

chapter 18

MY PYRAMID SCHEME

*You are stronger when you're
part of a strong, supportive team.*

BY SHAWNA BRANDNER

I WANT YOU TO think of a time when you had a great sense of accomplishment. Are you thinking about it now? Bask in the memory for a moment. Now, who did you celebrate with? If the answer is "a great team of people," or "a close group of friends," then you're on the right track. If the answer was "I was alone and no one celebrated," how did that make you feel? I can imagine that it was deflating, and that your elation at the accomplishment probably faded very quickly. You still accomplished something, but I bet it would have felt ten times better if you had a team to plan, collaborate, and celebrate with. I love my job! Everyone around me knows I love my job. I just can't help but be excited when I see what God is doing in people's lives. I feel privileged to work in a place where goals are accomplished and children are reached in ways I could never do by myself. God did not create man to be alone, so it doesn't make sense that you would do kidmin alone either. Excitement is contagious and if you spread it around, people will join in for the ride.

I can think of examples of times when I was flying solo in kidmin. On one occasion, I was setting up a new event we had never tried before. I was in charge of planning, shopping, setting up, and executing the event. I was the only person who was able to help out, so that meant I had to do everything by myself. The event came and went. It looked great and people had a good time, but in the end, I was left alone at my party for one and I didn't feel like celebrating. Even when people who attended told me what a great time they had, it just fell flat. I could not go to my team and excitedly relay the joy I felt at our event being well received. When it came time to decide on whether or not to hold that event again, there was no motivation to hold it. I didn't want to end up doing the whole thing alone a second time, so it just never happened again.

On the other hand, I can think of times when I should have felt overwhelmed or dismayed. So much needed to happen, and things were not going as planned, but in the end when everything came together there was a great sense of accomplishment and celebration. The difference was that I had a team of people there with me. We encouraged each other when things seemed bleak, helped each other troubleshoot problems, and celebrated as a group when we accomplished our goal. Instead of being discouraged by setbacks and a lack of time, I was motivated to do more because I was not alone. The shared experience of working with a team gives you something to celebrate and look forward to. It also gives you a reason to do something again, and perhaps even make it bigger, better, and more impactful. You're called as Christians to bear one another's burdens, and that applies to your ministry life as well.

Building a strong and supportive team takes you from a place of compromise to a place of success. It creates a place where people can use the gifts they were given by God to work together towards a common goal—a place where excellence is not compromised because there is a lack of motivation, knowledge, or skill. People were created to be different parts of the body of Christ, so you will be more successful when you fill in the places you lack with people who have those gifts.

"Now there are varieties of gifts, but the same Spirit; and there are varieties of service, but the same Lord; and there are varieties of activities, but it is the same God who empowers them all in everyone. To each is given a manifestation of the Spirit for the common good" (1 Corinthians 12:4-7, ESV).

If you have great administration skills, but you struggle with planning games, that's okay. God did not create you to be great at everything. What God did create is a beautiful reason to surround yourself with people who have different gifts than you. The best part is how excited people are to use the things they are good at in a meaningful way. The key is to match tasks to people's gifts and passions. It can take some time to figure out the best fit for each person, but the results make it worth the time and effort. It creates a group of dedicated people who have truly bought into what you're trying to accomplish, because you took the time to make the role or task a good fit. People are excited to use their gifts in an effective way, and you can do so much more with them than you can alone.

Having a strong and supportive team sets you up for success long term. You will risk burnout and dissatisfaction if you don't put a system in place that allows you to rest and regenerate. When you spend a large portion of your time feeding others, you will empty yourself much too quickly. Having a strong team means that someone has your back; with a team, there are competent individuals who can pick up the pieces in your absence. The one-man band may seem entertaining, but he is no replacement for the soul-lifting feeling of a full orchestra.

Ministry is hard, and if you're not careful it can be very lonely. I never thought that could happen to me, but it did. After a number of years of pouring everything I had into kidmin, without even realizing it, I was suddenly doing many tasks by myself. I made sets alone. I prepped materials for small groups alone. I dreamed about things we could do better, alone. And then there I was... alone.

What I was lacking was support and a team—one that worked together and celebrated accomplishments. Instead, I looked around desperate for connection that wasn't there. I poured myself into ministry and found that others around me did not have the same passion for it that I did. People served in the church, but their commitment started and ended each Sunday. I found myself pointing out the things I was doing to the people around me in a desperate attempt for some kind of affirmation or recognition. It was discouraging and became very lonely. It was time for a change. In my case, that change included God calling me into paid ministry at a different church. I'm not saying that's God's plan for you, but it was His plan for me. God showed me so much about people and how important community is. It is important to point out that teams are different sizes and each person on each team is different. It begins with you finding one other person who shares your passion for ministry. Think of it as building blocks. You add one block at a time, making sure each piece fits in place before you move onto the next block. It is so much healthier and way more sustainable long term.

In case you didn't catch it the first time, I want to restate the fact that ministry is hard. There are times of long hours. There are people who need you seven days a week sometimes. There are heartbreaking stories and emotional burdens. I don't say this to discourage you, but in an environment where I've seen the stress of scheduling almost take some people out of ministry, it's wise to make sure you're aware of the pitfalls and do all you can to avoid them.

This is where that strong supportive team comes in! They are the people who carry the burden alongside you. They pray with you and for you. They share the tasks and the stresses. They cry with you when a family in your church has some unthinkable tragedy strike them. They encourage you to rest when you need to, and help you with things when you feel bogged down. One of the things we do at my church is debrief after every Sunday and every event. It gives us all a chance, as a team, to look at the things that went well and celebrate them, and to acknowledge those who stepped up and worked hard. It also gives us the time to look at things we could have done better, and make plans to change things when necessary. Ministry is a marathon, not a sprint. It's important to have the right team in place so you can stay in the race for the long term. It may seem backwards, but sometimes staying in the race means that you have to slow down and consider adding a relay race component where you pass the baton to others so you have time to breathe and rehydrate.

When I think about what a strong and supportive team really means my mind keeps wandering to the phrase: "Oh the places you'll go." (Perhaps, it's the kid who lives inside me who goes to a Dr. Seuss book title, but I do work in kidmin.) When I took over the team I currently manage, I inherited a team of 100 complete strangers. My first goal was simple recognition. Can I run into a person from my team in Costco with my cartload of Goldfish, and recognize who they are? It was a struggle at first, and it took quite a bit of time. People dropped off the team, no-showed, and declined shifts. There was no loyalty to me, since I was this new person they had never met. It took almost a full year before I felt confident that I knew each of my people enough that if I saw them out of the church context I could tell you their name and something about them. Prior to that, it was more "I know your face and that you serve, but not your name." From there, relationships were built, and a solid team was formed. People stopped dropping out each term, let me know in advance if they could not make it, and some even found their own replacements! At this point, change can occur. People will step up and step into new roles as the team expands and works together.

Delegating responsibility and watching volunteers excel is one of my favorite things. God has moved and done amazing things with the team that I have, and He will do it for you, too. I don't always do the right thing or the best thing, but God has honored my commitment to always do the best I can with what I have in front of me. When I think of the structure as it was, with me holding up a team of 100 people, it was like an upside-down pyramid with all the blocks stacked on top of one point. I am not an engineer, but it would not take a ton of force to topple the whole thing. When you flip over the pyramid and share the load, the base of the pyramid is wider than the top and now it would take quite a bit of force to topple it. By developing people into support roles and having them excited about their part of the process, it takes the load off an individual's shoulders. Instead of having one person hold everything up, there is a foundation to carry the load. People who are part of the structure and really know which block God created them to be, stay invested and help to build the rest of the pyramid. The best part is, they are happy to do it! They are excited to be part of something that's bigger than them.

I'm excited because the people on my team have turned into the best recruiting force I have. Recruitment is not my strong suit. It's one area I am not gifted in, being the introvert that I am. But guess what? My team recruits people for me. That's the thing that makes me the most excited of all.

The change that God called me to was not the smoothest or the easiest transition, but it has been a valuable experience that has shown me just how great things can be with a support system and a team of people all working towards a common goal. It took work to get it where it is now, and it will take work to make it better from here. My team provides me with so many things: support, motivation, great ideas, accountability, relationship, growth, and a deeper appreciation of the people God has placed around me.

I like to think of this team as a well-oiled machine that has an exhaust output of joy. This machine has many parts. There are parts that cut and prep crafts, parts that create spreadsheets and do mail merges, parts that play with toys, parts that schedule and organize, parts that pray, parts that teach, parts that create branding and media, parts that write curriculum, parts that plan and execute events, parts that serve snacks. The result is excellent execution of Sundays and a group of people who find joy in serving the kingdom. Have you ever been somewhere when it's obvious that everyone just wants to get whatever it is done as quickly as possible and then leave? I know I have. I've also seen a group of people who just spent eight hours on their feet setting up, executing four services and tearing it all down, stand together to discuss the day with each other and hang out. Instead of rushing home, there is a celebration of what has been accomplished and a time to talk about things that hit us hard that day.

Being in kids' ministry can be both the most rewarding and the most challenging thing you can do. I have been both volunteer and paid ministry personnel and each has its own challenges. I don't know what position you're in, but I do know that no matter what, you will be stronger in a team than you will be alone. I'm excited to be in a position where I have a strong and supportive team working alongside me, but it has not always been that way. If you're doing ministry in a silo, I encourage you to build a strong and supportive team, because you will be so much stronger that way!

Shawna Brandner is career volunteer turned church staff, who loves strategy board games, sci-fi fantasy, and Diet Coke. She is a wife and a mother of 4 kids, all born 4 years apart in leap years, which just proves that God has a sense of humor.

chapter 19

THE GOOD PART

*You are stronger when you
see things from a differing perspective.*

BY RACHAEL GROLL

PEOPLE FILE PAST me on Sunday morning, and I struggle between feeling guilty and some sort of righteous indignation. We have close to 200 kids in the building, but my list of children's ministry volunteers continues to seem lackluster. We have some amazing and dedicated workers. Yet, as we continue to grow in our department, recruiting new helpers seems to be a daunting task. Our church has grown exponentially in recent years. The more we grow, the harder it seems to get people to sign on to help with one of the greatest ministries of the church—the few, the proud, the children's ministry. There's a sense that we have the corner on the one area of ministry that Jesus would definitely be in if He was serving in our church. I watch people walk out to their cars, realizing that I know most of them. If I don't know their names, I know their faces, and very few of them help in kidmin. It becomes very easy to get into this place of "Us vs. Them", especially when people say *no* to a personal invitation to help. Don't misunderstand, we have a large team of volunteers. They call us the chaos coordinators. I'm sure you've seen the hoodies and coffee mugs. Working in kidmin, there's always a pile of papers to file on your desk, a parent to call, the next event to plan. Your job is never done and sometimes that pressure can feel like a physical weight on your shoulders. If only there were more people to share the load and spread out the work, so it wasn't overwhelming. If only "they" would help "us."

I had the opportunity to help this month in a ministry other than kidmin. The food pantry was low on workers because of the flu, and I stepped in to help serve food to people in our community. When I walked up to the food pantry line, immediately my senses were assaulted with the smell of urine. Scanning the crowd of people, there was a sense of heartache as I assessed them.

There was an elderly man who was blind being escorted by one of our teens. They slowly trudged through the line, the man happy to get free carrots. Chuckling, he said something that made the teen laugh, and I watched how they seemed to enjoy a special kind of friendship. The teen, taking the box of food to the waiting car of the elderly man, waved goodbye to the caregiver with a promise to see them both next month.

There was a commotion behind me. When I turned to see what was happening, a woman I recognized from women's ministry tried to calm an elderly woman. The woman was cussing at the man behind her for saying something offensive. Her gravelly voice was suddenly strong as she explained to him what her husband would do to him if he spoke to her that way again. Our volunteer whispered something in her ear, and the woman's eyes twinkled as she offered a toothless grin of gratefulness. I heard her say, "Thank you, honey." She shuffled down the line along with her daughter, excitedly talking about the soup they are going to make for dinner.

A young mother pulled her children behind her in a faded plastic Little Tykes wagon. Two in the wagon and one in her arms, she already had her hands full. She collected the grape juice I offered, but didn't make eye contact. I watched her inch farther down the line, as the Lord quickly replaced any thoughts of inconvenience in the day's plans with compassion for the people in front of me. The young woman approached the end of the table. I watched as the volunteer not only got her to make eye contact, but was greeted with a warm smile. There's something familiar about the smile, although it takes a bit to place it. I looked down again at the wagon, and realized one of her children is a preschooler who had been at a weekend services. He came on one of the buses. He was familiar because I had to intervene with one of the classroom teachers due to his behavior. I realized the circumstances that brought this family to the food pantry may also be responsible for his behavior this past weekend. It brought a sickening feeling to the pit of my stomach.

Tears started to slip silently as the young mom walked away, and there was a gnawing at my heart as I watched her struggle. I left my post and chased after her. "Can I pray for you?" I heard myself say. Surprised, she looked up, made eye contact this time, with tears in her own eyes. "Yes, please," she responded. "My husband lost his job. This is all the food we have now." She struggled over her words. It's overwhelming to realize that God brought this woman to this moment, in order to allow me the opportunity to speak words of hope to her. I started to pray for her, and I realized that the volunteer who was speaking to her a moment before was suddenly at my side, a thoughtful hand of support on this young mom's shoulder. Looking up at us, she thanked us as she walked over to a tent that I hadn't seen before. Under the tent were thermoses of hot coffee, manned by a couple that I recognized from Sunday mornings. The young mom was given a word of encourage-ment with her hot coffee, and I watched her walk away, realiz-ing that she seemed a little bit lighter.

On the other hand, I seemed a little bit heavier. My heavy heart was not because of the weight of her situation, although it was heavy. The burden was actually conviction for not realizing the impact God was trying to make in our community through ALL of the ministries of our church... not just mine. Our church is placed for such a time as this, to meet the needs of the broken and hurting in our community. His plan to use me to minister to this young mom would have been missed if I were still back in my office, accomplishing my agenda. Instead, my obedience to meeting a need allowed me to see His agenda. Those few pre-cious moments gave me the opportunity to speak into the life of a family that otherwise I would not have been able to.

When you think about ministry in terms of how you are serv-ing, are you staying within your lane? Or are you looking and listening for opportunities to simply be obedient? This can be challenging. By the very nature of the role you are placed in, you are busy with lots of little hearts depending on you. However, if your heart is not dependent on Him, none of that will matter. A change in the posture of your heart can make all the difference. I watched our food pantry director walk up and down the aisles of food, while he greeted each volunteer by name. He asked about their families—about situations in their lives that he had been praying for. He is pastoring them. As I looked around at the number of children in the line, and the new faces serving them, I realized that there is no "Us vs. Them." It's just us. We're all on the same team. We're all working to advance the kingdom by serving people the way Jesus calls us to. I wonder if this team of faithful volunteers ever looks at me on a Sunday and wonders why I never help at the food pantry.

Contemplating the irony of the situation, I was drawn to a woman I recognized from church who is typically very quiet and reserved. She cleans the church, she sews snagged table-cloths, and she always helps in ways that are overlooked. But today, she declared peace over a family in line. She prayed over them in such a powerful way that I myself was encouraged. It reminded me of a verse that the Lord put on my heart very early on in ministry: *"And if you extract the precious from the worthless, You will become My spokesman"* (Jeremiah 15:19b, NASB).

I looked around at the people God sent us that day at the food pantry, and I realized that extracting the precious is precisely what was happening. God opened a door for ministry because of the faithful volunteers who see people the way God sees them, not the way the world does. I am so thankful for the people who love our community through this ministry. It grieves me to realize that my ignorance or inexperience of how vital that ministry is allowed me to judge their hearts when I saw them on Sundays. I wonder how many other people were serving in various ministries, and I didn't even know. Obviously, there are people who are not serving in any area, but it was so convicting for me to realize that my own attitude clouded my ability to see the ones who were.

The first step for me to become a spokesman for the Lord was answering the call to children's ministry. Sometimes, the never-ending number of tasks in ministry can lead to a side trail that can be very dangerous if not intentionally dealt with. Serving God is not about tasks. It's about people. Jesus calls you to serve because He loves people, and your primary role as a minister of the Gospel is to share that love with those He puts in your path. A familiar passage of scripture gives an example of how tasks can distract you from relationships and impact your attitude towards others in a similar way. In Luke 10, Jesus visited the home of Mary and Martha. Martha, overwhelmed by the number of tasks she had to complete, had a little bit of a familiar attitude towards her sister.

"But Martha was distracted with all her preparations; and she came up to Him and said, 'Lord, do You not care that my sister

has left me to do all the serving alone? Then tell her to help me.'
But the Lord answered and said to her, 'Martha, Martha, you
are worried and bothered about so many things; but only one
thing is necessary, for Mary has chosen the good part, which
shall not be taken away from her'" (Luke 10: 40-42, NASB).

Martha loved Jesus and worked tirelessly to accomplish what she thought were the most important tasks necessary in order to serve Him. Instead, He reminded her that the tasks were not the important thing. Her relationship with Him mattered more. A busy season of tasks can often result in very similar results. Focusing so much on what you need accomplished in order to do ministry can often get in the way of actual ministry. Sometimes, it takes stepping out of your ministry role to realize a renewed vision for what Jesus actually called you to. Jesus calls this the "good part." Are you getting the "good part"—the part where you hear the Lord and you are taking the time to sense His calling and purpose in your life? It can be so easy to get distracted from God's best for you, especially in ministry. As I served this month in a ministry other than my own, I was able to realize how my blinders kept me from seeing people and kept me focused on tasks. It's my prayer that you would be able to gain a little perspective from other ministries in your own church.

THINGS TO PONDER:

- Are there areas that you may have blinders on? What are you focused on right now? Does that, in any way, inhibit you from seeing people God has put in your path?

- What other areas in your church could you serve in, in order to gain some perspective in your own ministry areas?

- Are you getting time for what Jesus calls the "good part"?

CHALLENGE:

- Pray for God's agenda to trump your own agenda, allowing for moments that might otherwise escape the day.

Rachael Groll is the Children's and Outreach Pastor at Living Waters Church in Meadville, PA. Her book, *GO,* is a great resource for children's pastors who feel called to lead missional ministries. You can connect with her at SheHears.org

chapter 20

THE BEAUTY OF HEAVEN

*You are stronger when you
glorify God through diversity.*

BY JACE MARTIN

URING SPRING BREAK of my junior year of high school,
I went on a school-sponsored trip to France and Germany. One day, our tour guide gave us some free time
to wander around a quaint, little town in Germany. My friends
and I meandered from shop to shop repeating the few German
phrases we knew and enjoying the afternoon. At some point,
I realized that my friends had disappeared. (I don't totally remember how this happened, but I'm pretty sure my "friends"
ditched me.) Trying not to panic, I stepped out of the shop
and looked for them on the street. I checked all of the nearby
stores... gone. Increasingly frantic, I decided to return to the
bus, where we were supposed to meet at the specified time.

Unfortunately, I quickly discovered that I had no idea where the bus was located. I have a distinct memory of jogging down the street, smiling to avoid looking worried (as if a crazy, grinning foreigner jogging in blue jeans is the epitome of composure). As I prayed, I brainstormed ways to act out the phrase, "Help, my friends deserted me and I'm looking for a big bus!" I had no cell phone on me and had no way to get in touch with our tour guide or my teachers. Aside from excellent miming skills, I had no way to communicate with any storeowners or even law enforcement. I was completely on my own.

In a time when I was most vulnerable, I didn't know where to turn. In a time when I was most desperate, I had to keep my desperation to myself. In a time when I was most confused, there was nobody who understood me.

This is why diversity is so important in children's ministry. We have the opportunity to serve kids in some of their most impressionable times—when they're beginning to discover their own identity. All metaphors or illustrations break down, and mine does quickly, because I cannot claim to understand the difficulties faced by people in true minority situations. My moment of panic is incomparable to the lifetime of struggles they face. But maybe you can relate. Maybe there was a time you knew you didn't belong. And in that moment, you got an ever-so-small glimpse at how some kids might feel in your ministry.

Your church likely has kids who come from all kinds of backgrounds. How can you minister to all of them and show them they belong? In this chapter, we will explore what diversity is, why it's important in children's ministry, and things you can do to improve diversity in your own church.

WHAT IS DIVERSITY?

Diversity is simply a variety. In terms of social diversity, it describes a group comprised of people from different cultural backgrounds, ethnicities, ages, and experiences. Diversity is not something that passively occurs. It takes concerted effort; it does not "just happen."

Perhaps when you read the word *diversity* your first thought was racial or ethnic diversity. Nowadays in American culture, this is an important topic of discussion. In fact, ethnic diversity is an area in which the American Church (including my church) has a lot of work to do. The goal of racial or ethnic diversity is not to homogenize all people groups to behave the same way. It is to incorporate all the experiences, perspectives, and ideas of different ethnicities to benefit the whole body of Christ.

In children's ministry, gender diversity is also critical, but the issues the church faces are the opposite of what most other organizations face. If you have too many males serving in your children's ministry, please raise your hand. Oh, nobody? No children's ministry I've been a part of has too much testosterone. At first glance, this might seem like a minor issue. However, this is something to be taken seriously. Yes, kids need to learn from women, but they also need to learn from men. Kids benefit from seeing the qualities of God displayed by both genders. Picture your fourth and fifth-grade boys. Do they see men volunteering, worshipping, and teaching? Are they being shown what it means to be a Christian man? Picture your young girls. Do they have an example of what a godly man should look and act like? There are a lot of worldly messages being given to young kids about what a man should be, and many of those messages are alarming. Kids need to know what Christian adults look like, both men and women.

Diversity can also refer to age. Those who are older than you have wisdom and experience that are infinitely valuable. I'm a young pastor, so sometimes I think I know the coolest, most innovative ways to do things. Admittedly, I can have tunnel vision. Internally, I ask a lot of questions about how to improve, like, "How can we do this better?" "What would make this cooler?" "What's the freshest way to accomplish this task?"

However, I have benefited greatly from veteran volunteers who have spent years and years in our ministry. They have seen an abundance of change, both good and bad, and have the ability to slow me down with their wisdom. On the other hand, younger perspectives help ministries grow. They show you where you've become stagnant and give you new ideas. When your ministry has a broad range of ages, you're able to see situations from every angle.

Have you ever heard of an echo chamber? It describes the phenomenon where an entire group of people only encounters beliefs or ideas that agree with their own. Everyone shares their opinions, but they agree with each other, so they just echo louder and louder and nothing changes—you don't change. Your own ideas—even if they're incorrect or misplaced—are reinforced and strengthened. This is what you're trying to avoid. To be diverse, you want to hear and consider differing opinions and perspectives.

WHY IS DIVERSITY IMPORTANT?

It's a picture of heaven.

Revelation 7:9-10 (NIV) says,

> *"After this I looked, and behold, a great multitude that no one could number, from every nation, from all tribes and peoples and languages, standing before the throne and before the Lamb, clothed in white robes, with palm branches in their hands, and crying out with a loud voice, 'Salvation belongs to our God who sits on the throne, and to the Lamb!'"*

Heaven is going to be the most beautifully diverse gathering of people ever. Every time you worship with those who belong to a different people group, you experience the beauty and wonder of heaven. Jesus prayed in Matthew 6 for God's Kingdom to come on earth as it is in heaven. When you practice diversity, you're bringing more of God's heavenly kingdom to earth. Paul set an example in this. In Galatians 3:28, he encourages the church in Galatia to put aside their spiritual racism. There was a sect of Jewish Christians who believed that it was necessary to follow the Old Testament law in order to be a believer. This was causing strife between the Jewish believers and the Gentile converts to Christianity. It is through this situation that there is a poetic turn of phrase by Paul: *"There is neither Jew nor Greek, there is neither slave nor free, there is no male and female, for you are all one in Christ Jesus"* (Galatians 3:28, NIV). Paul doesn't encourage the Gentile believers to form their own church, and he doesn't encourage the Jewish believers to excommunicate the Gentile believers. Instead, he points to their unity under the banner of Christ Jesus. Each time you put unity in Jesus above differences in ethnicities and backgrounds, you get to see an awesome picture of heaven.

It's a gift from God.

1 Corinthians 12:12 (NIV) says, *"Just as a body, though one, has many parts, but all its many parts form one body, so it is with Christ."* And then later, in 12:18, *"But in fact God has placed the parts in the body, every one of them, just as he wanted them to be."* Our differences are something that should be celebrated and utilized. Everyone has a role to play. Everyone has something to bring to the table. For instance, a person of color has a set of experiences and perspectives that others don't. When you ignore this, you ignore one of the clearest ways God has gifted His Church.

In fact, this is demonstrated in the triune nature of God. Each member of the Trinity plays a role, but they are unified. The Father is the creator, the Son is the savior, and the Spirit is the counselor. Or, in other words, the Father created us and the plan, the Son fulfilled the plan, and the Spirit continues to administer the plan. Our diversity and ability to play different roles is a direct reflection of the nature of God.

It shows a variety of people that they belong.

It's a well-known phenomenon that congregations will generally reflect their leadership. Do this experiment: next Sunday, look around your main worship service. How many of the congregants are the same race and general age as your preaching pastor? If yours is like many churches, they are very similar. Or, maybe you've heard a sentiment like this: "Worship wasn't very good today. I wish we did more of [fill in the blank with the preferred style of musical worship]." Though perhaps a selfish and inappropriate view of musical worship, the average church-goer will rarely stay at a church in which they don't feel they belong. And can you blame them? You naturally want to put yourself in situations where you belong.

A couple of weeks ago, I walked a visiting family with a third-grade boy, John, to his room. Though he didn't appear nervous, John definitely didn't look thrilled to be at church. I explained our check-in system and how our programming works, when I was interrupted by John's excited yells. "Mom!" he said, "That kid is in my class at school!" Immediately, John shot into the room.

John's behavior is normal. He saw someone he knew and quickly recognized that this is a place he wanted to be. Humans innately understand when they belong somewhere. Have you ever watched an 18-month-old enter the nursery? Nobody needs to explain that the toys are for them. It's your job to create situations and environments where every child, volunteer, and parent—no matter where they come from or what they look like—knows they belong.

So, where do you go from here?

Again, diversity does not occur without a concerted effort. You have to work at it. So, the first step that I recommend is to surround yourself with people from different backgrounds. Do you have a parent committee? (This is slightly off-topic, but if you don't have a parent committee/panel/ roundtable that meets regularly and provides input, I would highly recommend creating one!) If so, make sure there are people from a variety of walks of life. Invite people who are younger than you, older than you, of a different ethnicity, from a different faith background, or of a different gender. Invite people who are going to disagree with you. Invite people who will push back on your ideas. Perhaps, if I may sound crazy for a second, invite people you don't like! (Are you allowed to admit that you don't get along well with some people?) Invite people who have a different perspective than you.

Here's the problem: when you only look from your perspective, you miss things. One Sunday, I led our weekly pre-service meeting for volunteers. We went through prayer requests, talked through the curriculum for the day, and answered questions. Right after we dismissed, Jessica, the Early Childhood Coordinator at our church, came up to me and tapped me on the shoulder. "Jace," she whispered, "you have a hole in your pants." I looked down at my favorite pair of khakis, and sure enough, there was a hole in a place you definitely don't want a hole.

Was I embarrassed in the moment? Of course. Did I immediately call my wife and ask her to bring me another pair? You bet. Did I wish that Jessica had told me that tidbit before I led the meeting? Would have been nice. But above all, I was grateful that Jessica felt comfortable enough to tell me this information.

Maybe you've been in this situation. Maybe you've been told you have broccoli in your teeth, or that your fly is unzipped, or that you've been calling someone by the wrong name. It hurts a little. For a second, you're embarrassed, and (if you're like me) even mad at the person who pointed it out to you. But when you have a chance to think about it, you're probably grateful. Because you can't see what you can't see.

This is how you should approach conversations about diversity. You might hear some things you don't want to hear. You might hear that you have not fostered an environment where those in an ethnic minority feel comfortable. You might hear that you have acted offensively. And you have to be okay with that and do better next time.

This is how you build trust. These individuals need to know that you welcome their input, even if it's critical in nature. If you ignore their perspectives, you appear two-faced and fake. It looks like you're checking a box.

Then, you need to put a variety of people in positions of exposure in your ministry. Again, because you know congregations often reflect whoever is in front of them, you should take advantage of this. Is there a volunteer who has shown potential in teaching? Could you add some diversity to your new families team? Is there someone with musical abilities who might want to help with worship? It's incredibly valuable for kids to see people of all races and backgrounds in front of them.

As you probably guessed, I eventually found the bus in the small town in Germany. (Did you think I was writing this from Europe?) I eventually found what I needed. Similarly, there is hope for kids in your ministry. There are ways for you to help everyone feel welcome. I don't know of a single kidmin leader who doesn't want all kids to feel welcome in his or her ministry. I know that you all want to foster an environment of inclusion. So, be proactive in allowing the beauty of heaven to be reflected in your ministry.

Jace Martin and his wife, Kendall, live in Colorado Springs, where he serves as the Children's Pastor at Pikes Peak Christian Church. He enjoys coaching basketball, reading, and playing games with friends.

chapter 21

LIKE POPCORN AT THE MOVIES

You are stronger when all children are included.

BY STACY MARKS

M Y FAMILY LOVES to go to the movies. To be quite honest, with three boys at home, ages 8 and under, I usually only go to the theater to see the newest animated release (not to say that I mind). But whenever we go, there's one thing that cannot be missed—the popcorn! I mean, a movie's just better with popcorn, don't you think? I don't care if it's kettle corn, or butter. There's just something about sitting down to a movie, relaxing in the chair, and snacking on hot fresh popcorn. In my family, obviously, we get a large, because in our town, that means a free refill! Our motto is "Eat up... there's more where this came from!"

It's time for the truth... the hard truth. When I stop and think about it, after I've indulged in handful after handful of popcorn... well... I don't really like popcorn. Popcorn is, in fact, very irritating to me. Popcorn always, without fail, gets stuck between my teeth in the worst way. The kernels in my teeth are painful. Sometimes it takes days after flossing and brushing and rinsing to be rid of all the kernels! As I'm walking out of the movies I always think, "Next time, I'm going to stick to the candy and skip the popcorn. The popcorn is just not worth it!" But then we head to the next movie, I walk in, and I know for sure that this movie, despite my last experience, will be better with popcorn. And, yes, we buy the large. We plan for a refill, and we sit and enjoy the movie! Even after all that irritation with the kernels, I cannot be convinced that a movie can be watched without popcorn!

I bet you have a kid in your ministry who is like popcorn. You know, the kid who walks in the door to your class and your heart beats a little harder, and your brain spins with all the possibilities she could be up to today. It's the kid who after you clean up, lock up, and start walking to the car you think, "Never again." "Next week he will sit with his parents." "Next week I will have to tell her mom this is just not working out." "I just cannot do this anymore." "Next week..." You can fill in the blank. I will not sit here and write this chapter and pretend I've never had these thoughts. On my best day, I take a deep breath and give it to Jesus, but sometimes I walk out of a Sunday and think, "I've had enough!"

And then, just like that popcorn at the movies, the next week comes, and the child comes back, and I smile. I smile, because I know we can do it. I smile, because I hope today might be different. I smile, because I believe we are stronger, and my kids' ministry is better when everyone is included. No matter how irritating the child may be, no matter the struggle all week to "get the kernels out of my teeth" and come up with a new plan, I believe the church... that class... this ministry... it's just better when everyone is included. The movie is always better with the popcorn.

As I've dealt with those "popcorn" kids, there are two particular groups that stand out to me, that can give churches ministry challenges. These are children with special needs, and children who have experienced trauma or are coming from hard places. I believe you need to take special care to include these children, but also, make adaptations and changes to your ministry so that every child, no matter what their needs or background is, can be included. Every child is worth it! Every child needs Jesus.

INCLUDING KIDS WITH SPECIAL NEEDS

The world *inclusion* is often used in the world of special education. You hear things like: full inclusion and partial inclusion. This describes when a child is included in a classroom of regularly developing children. Laws in most states dictate that students with special needs (who often have IEPs—Individualized Educational Programs—that are focused on the learning needs and goals for a particular student) have the right to be provided with a public education in the least restrictive environment.

What does this mean for the church? That law is for public education. Often, I hear it's hard for families with children of special needs to attend church, because they're afraid or cannot drop off their children. Many churches have special programs, or even sensory rooms, for children with special needs. But I also understand that not every church is equipped with the resources to be able to make a program like this happen. They simply don't have any room for dedicated space for something like a sensory room.

Because we are stronger together, and because every child deserves to be able to come to church and worship and hear about the living God, you run a full inclusion classroom. You have chosen to partner with parents to make your classrooms manageable for a variety of special needs. This is done on a case-by-case basis. You have kids with autism, Down syndrome, and other learning disabilities and physical needs. Because of your belief that you are better together, you have designed a learning environment where everyone can be involved.

Partnering with the parents is always the best way to help a child succeed. Let them know you want to include their child. Meet with the parents to get to know them and their child better. Keep open communication with them and ask for help whenever you need it. Don't forget to celebrate the child's victories each week!

INCLUDING KIDS FROM HARD PLACES

If you've never done any research on the results of trauma on the brain, might I recommend that this is your next read. Childhood experiences, both positive and negative, have tremendous impact on the brain and behavior of children. Negative experiences, called ACES (Adverse Childhood ExperienceS) have a critical impact on behavior, lifelong health, and other negative outcomes in the life of an individual. As ministers of the Gospel of Jesus, you must become more aware of the current studies of trauma, and more effectively and patiently, teach and minster to kids from hard places. Many children today are living in a world that is not safe for them. You and your church may be the only place of safety and peace they experience on a weekly basis. You are stronger when you become a safe haven for all children. These children need you. Most importantly, these children need Jesus.

Children from hard places can most easily be identified in your ministry when they have come from foster care or adoption. Please be gentle and supportive with these families as they care for the needs of orphans. That in and of itself is a special calling. But, ACES can also be seen in seemingly typical families. A death of a loved one, a parent or family member struggling with addiction or depression, and many other situations can have effects on a child, even from the most "normal" of families. Be sensitive and make everyone feel loved. Understand trauma and its effect on the brain. You will be stronger, and your ministry will be stronger because of it.

INCLUDE EVERYONE

Special needs children and children from hard places are just some of the children in your ministry with specific needs. But there are all kinds of kids in your ministry! There are kids with discipline problems, kids who just had a bad morning, kids from different cultural backgrounds, kids with food allergies, kids with big opinions, shy kids, loud kids, class clown kids... kids, kids, kids!

My goal in ministry is that all kids are included, connected, have fun, and learn about Jesus. But to do that and manage all types of behavior and needs is challenging! I am constantly changing our program and making adaptations to make it the best it can be for every child.

My own children have taught me a lot about adapting my programs so that everyone is included. Caleb, my 8-year-old, is very easy-going, but can be painfully shy, and needs an adult around to feel safe. Because I know he's not the only child like that, I've made sure we have adequate ratios in our elementary ministry, so that every child can be known by a safe and trusted adult. I also make sure to have lots of free time activities that are self-directed, for kids who need some alone time before engaging with a group. Joshua, my 5-year-old, can be a challenging child. He struggles with fine motor skills and doesn't always love crafts, because they're not fun; they are literally hard for him to accomplish. He's not the only child who struggles in this way, so I've made sure that our activity time can be adapted for kids who struggle with writing or scissors. These adaptations are easily made by providing some labels with preprinted words, and having several crafts pre-cut for children.

Being mindful of who you are ministering to, and making adaptations for them is difficult, but rewarding, because when you do this, everyone can be included. Everyone feels like they belong! Here are some questions and ideas to help you start thinking about including every child. Hopefully, it gives you some thoughts on making your program stronger.

- Does a child need a one-on-one aide to help them with activities? Pray for help in this area if that is the case. Yes, it does mean scheduling one more volunteer... but it's worth it! (Make sure it's the right volunteer for the child.)

- Think through your ratios. Are you struggling with discipline? Do you need a better active adult:child ratio in your classroom?

- Discipline strategy. Are you only pointing out what is wrong? Are you telling children what they did right?

- Get on their level. Are you greeting a child and making eye contact with them? Do you know their name? (It's okay to use name tags!) When a child comes in who is shy or struggling, get down on their level, but take a knee and handle them gently.

- Transitions can be hard for any child. Are the transitions in your classroom smooth? Can you give children a longer warning, before an activity ends so they can "close the loop" on what they're doing?

- Welcoming shy children into your classroom can be challenging. Try getting them interested in an activity or project. Can you give them a unique gift (smelly sticker, special pen or marker, special bracelet or even a craft challenge) to help them enter your room well?

- Never ask a child to read out loud; only take volunteers for such an activity. This avoids any awkward situations for a child with any learning disability.

- Think through crafts and activities. Does your activity add frustration for a child who struggles with fine motor development? How can it be modified? Can you give options of activities, instead of one set activity, so a child can do what is most comfortable? Is your activity too simple for older children? Can you make an adaptation for those children?

- Are you teaching to all the learning styles (visual, auditory, and kinesthetic)? Are there creative changes you can make in your lesson delivery so all children can learn?

- Worship. Is it too loud? Is there an option for children to move if the noise is hard for them? Can children read the words on the screen? Can you help children learn a new song in a new way?

- Look into fidget tools and sensory input activities to help all kids succeed.

- How are you communicating with parents? Do they know your needs? Are you partnering with them appropriately to have a successful classroom? Think about a daily report card, especially for younger kids, so you can tell parents what their child enjoyed and how they did.

WE ARE BETTER TOGETHER

I know this is a hard subject. I know many of you have just come off a Sunday where you have had a child press every possible button, and some buttons you didn't even know you had! I am with you... 1000% with you (yes, not 100%, literally a thousand!) I, too, have had kids hide under tables. I have had kids tell me they don't have to listen to me. I have been kicked and bitten. I've seen a thousand eye rolls. Two weeks ago, I even had a special needs student lay on the bathroom floor and refuse to get up. I am in the trenches with you, friend. But weekly, I also smile, because I know, that despite the hard work, full-on sprints through classrooms, numerous talks and prayers, we are better, we are stronger, when everyone, is included. Remember... the movie is always better with the popcorn.

Stacy Bingham Marks is the proud momma to 3 boys—Caleb the brave, Joshua the strong, and the amazing Benjamin. She is a self-proclaimed Disneyland expert and a glamping enthusiast. She and her husband, McKenzie, live in Napa, CA, where she is children's pastor at Hillside Christian Church, to which she is thankful for their support and vision to reach the next generation!

chapter 22

FROM CHAOS TO CONTROL

*You are stronger when you have
effective time management.*

BY RACHEL PRICE

I T'S A DAILY STRUGGLE to get my daughter to make her bed
in the morning. For some reason, she chooses to wait until
bedtime to complete the task and then complains it doesn't
make sense, because she's just going to mess it up again. It's great
when she finally obeys, but by the time she's waited all day, it los-
es its effectiveness. She's done the right thing, but in the wrong
time. There is no right time to do the wrong thing, but there is a
wrong time to do the right thing. It's important to manage your
time so the right things are being done at the right time.

I am stronger when I have good time management—as a
leader, team member, parent, or spouse. This applies to each
area of life. The Bible commands us, *"... be careful how you live.*

Don't live like fools, but like those who are wise. Make the most of every opportunity in these evil days. Don't act thoughtlessly, but understand what the Lord wants you to do" (Ephesians 5:15-17, NLT).

In the original text, it says to *redeem*, meaning to ransom or rescue from loss. You have to be intentional to rescue your time from distractions. You can easily lose the time you don't intentionally redeem. I'm often reminded, if the enemy can't destroy you, he will try to distract you. These distractions come in all forms.

Stay alert: good things can be distractions from the right thing. Just because you're doing good things, doesn't mean you're doing what you're supposed to do. With so many important things to be done in so little time, how do you determine what gets done when?

Time management is not a matter of whether there is enough time in the day, it's a question of how the time is spent. God makes every single day. He purposely gives just the amount of time needed to complete what He has planned for you in each day.

So, how do you know what the Lord wants you to do with that time? How do you identify the right thing and the right timing? Over the course of this chapter I will highlight five steps to effective time management: Prayer, Planning, Priorities, Productivity, and Purpose.

PRAYER

The first and most important step in managing time is making sure it's used correctly. Start each day by asking God what He has planned for you. Just because something is on your to-do list does not mean it's on God's. Are you doing what God has outlined for you in the time He has prescribed?

You are promised that God has good plans for you and He wants you to prosper. This means if you follow His designed steps and plans, you will be effective and successful. Ask God what His to-do list is for your time. Seek His wisdom, creativity, and guidance, then let God download His ideas as you plan ahead.

PLANNING

Benjamin Franklin said, "By failing to plan, you are planning to fail." If you want to have strong time management, you have to look ahead. I plan my time in four portions: yearly, seasonally, weekly, and daily. I look at the big picture and work backward.

Plan out the full year before it starts. Meet with key team members in July to start plans for the following year. What events will take place and what's the most effective time for each event? As you do this, consider holidays, special events, and how attendance is affected by each. Spend a couple of months prayerfully considering what God wants to accomplish in the coming year. By September, have the events finalized and loaded into your calendar.

Next, look at each season. Plan the details for each event one season in advance. In season one month one, finalize plans for season two month one. Season one month two will be spent detailing out season two month two, and so forth. Since the event has already been determined, this planning time is more efficiently used to iron out the details. With this system in place, preparing is less stressful, which allows for more creativity and enjoyment.

While planning the details, set dates and reminders on your calendar as to when items need to be addressed. When should you start promotion for an event? What is the deadline for having team members identified? When do supplies need to be ordered to allow plenty of time for preparation? This process will take time up front, but will save time in the long run.

Once all this is done, you should be able to zero in on the month you're entering. What is the big goal this month? What has to be accomplished? What would you like to accomplish? It's important to do this in each stage of planning. Know before you start your month, your week, your day what you *hope* to do, and what you *must* do.

Planning ahead is a key part of managing your time. Having a clear vision of where you're going makes the trip more enjoyable for yourself and those you are leading. Once you know the plans, prioritize the steps for accomplishing them.

PRIORITIES

Write out what needs to be done and assign a priority number to each task. Then, sort your list accordingly. Creighton Abrams said, "When eating an elephant take one bite at a time." Whether it be a growing ministry, parenting, marriage, or life in general, don't allow an overwhelming calendar to get you down. Tackle it one day, one task, one minute at a time.

Split your list into segments and assign deadlines. What has to be done this morning? What can be done this afternoon? What can wait until another day? Assign "another day" items to a specific date, so they don't fall off the calendar.

Be realistic when setting timelines. It's easy to set goals and fail to properly allow for how long a task will take. Plan for the unexpected. Life is full of interruptions, so allow time for them. Any parent knows it will take more than two minutes to get the kids into the car and back out of the driveway. There seems a be a correlation between an adult saying, "It's time to leave" and a child needing to go to the bathroom. They always want to wait until the exact second they are buckled into the car to remember they had to go potty the whole time. Then, their mind is suddenly jolted and they remember they're also starving. As a mom, I know this is going to happen, and add cushion to my departure time so it's not rushed.

Things will come up that you do not have written on your calendar. Leave room in your schedule for taking phone calls from parents, making emergency hospital visits, and other unexpected needs. Write these things into your calendar as they occur. This will help you to both stay accountable for your time, and realize how often the unexpected really happens.

As you plan your time, put the most important items at your most productive time of day. A morning person should not be writing lessons in the afternoon. Likewise, a night owl should not be trying to plan a large event first thing in the morning. Look ahead and plan this portion of your calendar to help your time be spent in the most effective way possible. Once you're done identifying your tasks and planning your time, focus on how you can be most productive.

PRODUCTIVITY

You can plan all day, but if you don't put it into action, it's a waste. However, looking at the list of tasks, even after they've been broken down, can still be overwhelming. There are a few things you can do to reduce the level of stress this will produce.

Delegate: You are not expected to do this alone. You are stronger when you include others. Let other people be a part of what God is doing. Share the vision with them, equip them, and allow them to be blessed as they use their God-given talents to help in the mission.

Do what only you can do: You are not the only one who can turn on lights. You are not the only one who can cut out crafts. What is it that only you can do? Focus on those things and delegate the rest.

Decision-making: Make decisions at the most efficient level. Once you have strong people in place to help with the planning, preparation, and execution, give them the authority to make decisions that directly affect them. Allowing other people to have input not only helps you see things from a different perspective, it gives team members ownership, which helps them buy into the vision.

Time management is more about team building and delegation than it is manipulating time. One person cannot possibly do it all. Surround yourself with others who are passionate about the calling and support the vision. As you and your team plan and prepare, remember to keep focus on your purpose.

PURPOSE

Why are you doing what you are doing? Identify the *why* and get passionate about it. Your passion will produce purpose in the people around you, and purpose produces productivity.

Everything should be done "... *heartily, as to the Lord, and not unto men*" (Colossians 3:23, KJV). The ultimate goal is to glorify God. Within that objective, what other purpose does your task serve? If you don't know where you're going, how will you know when you arrive? If you don't know what you're doing, how will you know when you're done? If you don't know why you're doing something, what will motivate you to continue? Go back to why.

Is your purpose to grow a children's ministry that will produce lifelong followers of Christ? Are you putting on this event to bring people into church? If so, how many?

Identify measurables. How will you know when you hit the target? Are you just trying to survive camp, or are you passionate about bringing as many kids as possible so they can encounter a life-changing week like no other? Is Christmas just a busy season when you see the once-a-year Christians? Or is it an opportunity to share with people who may otherwise have forgotten there is a God who loves them and cares about them no matter what? Answer these questions, and share with your team. Help them get passionate about what God is doing by showing the purpose in all of it. Make sure it is His purpose, not your own.

With a million and one things vying for your attention, ultimately you are the one who will choose which things win. Be disciplined and intentional in what you allow to have your time and attention. Does it add value? Is it beneficial? Is it part of the big picture? What role does it play in your purpose, priorities, and productivity?

As you follow these 5 Ps of time management, you'll notice you are stronger as a leader, a minister, and an individual. Be intentional with your time and invest it in people and things that will benefit your purpose.

Be accountable for your time. It is a gift. Each person is allotted just enough time to do what God has placed them here to do. You don't get to decide how much time you will be given, but you do get to decide how you will spend the time you are given. Choose wisely.

This is a choice you will make every day. As you are praying and planning, ask God to make clear His priorities and purpose in everything you do. Ask Him to bring the people who will help you be most productive.

As Jesus told His disciples, *"The harvest is plentiful but the workers are few. Ask the Lord of the harvest, therefore, to send workers into his harvest field"* (Matthew 9:37-38, NIV). This is His harvest, His ministry, His plan, His time. God will provide. You must simply ask.

Pray, plan, and prepare. When you do these things, you will be stronger and more productive as you follow God's purpose. When my daughter finally learns to make her bed in the morning, she will reap the many benefits of that preparation and planning throughout her day. Likewise, as you follow the 5 Ps of time management, you will enjoy the rewards. It is so refreshing to feel prepared and productive as everything is covered in prayer, planned ahead, and purpose-driven.

Rachel Price is an author, speaker, consultant, and Children's Ministries Pastor in Bentonville, AR. She is a wife, mom, and fan of all things coffee. For more information, visit rachelprice.com.

chapter 23

PLANNING FOR PROSPERITY

*You are stronger when you
have an overview of the year.*

BY DR. KRISTY MOTTE

EVERYONE'S BEEN THERE. Saturday night ... 10pm ... kids are in bed. You're winding down for the evening and then suddenly you realize, *I'm supposed to teach tomorrow!* You rack your brain for ideas, browse some free lessons online, and then head to your favorite social media children's ministry site to ask other kidmin leaders what they have planned for the morning. Maybe you find a stellar idea, maybe you don't. If all else fails? You win over the hearts of your kids and play a review game or show a movie.

There's certainly nothing wrong with a movie now and then and review games are an excellent way to reinforce what your group is learning, but is there a better way?

Solomon, gifted with wisdom straight from the Heavenly Father, has this reminder, *"Good planning and hard work lead to prosperity, but hasty shortcuts lead to poverty"* (Proverbs 21:5, NLT). Clearly, no one is called to kidmin to become rich, but I think Solomon's idea of prosperity has a deeper application for those in ministry. As a kidmin leader, you're making spiritual investments into the lives of those the Lord has entrusted you to shepherd. You are called to be a good steward of that investment, working for prosperity and following Solomon's advice to avoid poverty. Be aware church leader. The poverty at stake is not an empty bank account; instead, it's a destitute 6-year-old facing a bully at school or a spiritually bankrupt tween facing an onslaught of worldly temptation as he or she prepares for middle school. Man, what a high calling the Lord has deemed *you* fit for. He chose *you* to champion their spiritual development and to nurture their souls. What an honor!

So, what is the better way? How can you make sure the storehouses of the hearts of that 6-year-old or almost teenager is overflowing with spiritual riches? How can you practically implement Solomon's wise advice for planning and hard work? Ultimately, kidmin worker, you are stronger when you have a plan for the upcoming year. Spirit-led direction and intentional planning should be the backbone of your children's ministry.

You might be thinking, "An entire year?" The prospect of such an undertaking might seem overwhelming at first, but it doesn't have to be. In fact, there are really six core principles to consider when planning your year in children's ministry.

#1: BEGIN IN PRAYER

The first key to planning the year for your children's ministry is to start with prayer. Remember the goal? Spirit-led direction and intentional planning are only possible when you wait on the direction of the Father. He knows the hearts and needs of the kids you teach. He knows what they will face this year.

He knows HIS heart for their salvation, discipleship, and future. And He wants to grow His kingdom. Let Him take the lead. He promises, *"For everyone who asks, receives. Everyone who seeks, finds. And to everyone who knocks, the door will be opened"* (Luke 11:10, NLT). Ask the Lord where He's moving and to help you move with Him. Look at the needs of your group and ask for His direction.

#2: HAVE THE END IN MIND

Okay. I know I asked you to plan for the year, but what if... just for a second... you thought a little bigger? As you plan for the year, consider what the goal of your ministry is.

In the past, I've spent time in the elementary school classroom. As a teacher in secular education, you're constantly reminded to hit the targets of national standards and that your students will need to be equipped to pass their state standardized tests. The classroom teacher knows that the long-term goal involves high school graduation (and perhaps beyond) and that getting there involves everything from meeting yearly goals, semester or term goals, and even the objectives or goals for individual daily lessons. In kids' ministry, there aren't formal assessments or government mandated standards (praise the Lord!), but it can be helpful to consider what you hope the "product" of your ministry will be.

Paul writes to the church in Philippi, a body of believers he loved deeply:

"I pray that your love will overflow more and more, and that you will keep on growing in knowledge and understanding. For I want you to understand what really matters, so that you may live pure and blameless lives until the day of Christ's return. May you always be filled with the fruit of your salvation—the righteous character produced in your life by Jesus Christ—for this will bring much glory and praise to God" (Philippians 1:9, NLT).

Paul's heart for those he so affectionately cared for is a great "end" goal for the ministry leader. May those you shepherd:

- Overflow with the love, knowledge, and understanding of the Lord
- Live pure and blameless lives
- Embody the fruit of the Spirit as those who have truly become new in Christ
- Live lives that bring glory and praise to the Father.

As you begin planning the more specific ins and outs of the year, come back to this list or your own "end goals" often. Ask, "Does this (whatever it is you're planning) work towards accomplishing these goals?" If not, refocus it or rejoice in the ability to scrap it and replace it with something that is kingdom-focused and intentional.

#3: HIT THE HIGHS

The church calendar is filled with amazing opportunities to foster exciting ministry opportunities that will potentially be the "highs" of your year. They might even be the highs of the year for the children and leaders in your ministry. Rather than feeling you're interrupting the flow of the year with big holidays and events, start planning your year with them in mind. The highs to hit may vary according to your context, but some to consider are Easter, the end of the school year, your summer camp or VBS, the start of school, and Christmas.

As you consider what the highs of your ministry will be, you don't necessarily have to identify what the big event or lesson around that time will be. Do think about what you might want to focus on or how what you're teaching around that time can prepare the hearts of your kids for what that time of year means. For instance, when school starts, you might want to remind kids that their classroom at school is a mission field, that followers of the Lord are called to do everything with all of their heart as unto the Lord (even homework!), and that showing respect to their teacher, even when others don't, honors the Lord. Some curricula might call these "bottom lines" or "big ideas of the day." They're simply the take-away ideas you want kids to leave with because of their time with you in the Word.

#4: GET ORGANIZED

Without organization, your brainstorming session about the milestones of ministry for the next year can be wasted in mere moments. Benjamin Franklin said, "For every minute spent organizing, an hour is earned." As you work, do so with a method of organization that will save you time and energy in the future. After all, what good is planning your whole year if you can't find the plans later? It's terribly frustrating to have a super great idea and then not be able to remember it later. I know organization isn't everyone's favorite, but the good news is that you can use whatever system works for you. Do you work through primarily electronic means? Begin with a calendar on your computer noting the big events for the coming year. Add notes to the events with the ideas you come up with in your brainstorming session. Not a computer person when it comes to brainstorming or schedules? Use your planner, print out a blank calendar and write in notes, or get a giant dry erase calendar for your office. Do you like the file system? Label hanging file holders with the months of the year and then insert a file for each event into its corresponding month. In the file, keep your notes, ideas, flyers, or anything else you'd like. The bottom line? There's no right way to organize, but organization provides a structure that is incredibly helpful long term.

5: FILL IN (MOST OF) THE BLANKS

Once you have a general idea of the highs in your ministry, and you have an organization system in place that works for you, start filling in the weeks that remain on your calendar. First, do you know of any times you won't have children's ministry? Do you break for summer? Take spring break off? Integrate family Sundays? When you know dates like these ahead of time, add them to your calendar and factor them into your plan. That way, you're not blindsided later on and facing the choice to combine weeks, skip over a concept, or push the entire schedule back a week.

As you fill in the blanks for the rest of the year, consider your context. Do you use a purchased curriculum? If so, grab its scope and sequence and plot their themes out on your calendar for the year. You'll be surprised how the Holy Spirit will prep your own heart over the coming months for the different topics your kids will encounter. If you write your own curriculum, look at the themes you have in mind for the year and potentially how long that theme will take. You can then evaluate your calendar to see where that concept best fits. For instance, I tend to organize themes around months. Three to five weeks is generally long enough to reinforce a big idea for mastery without the risk of exhausting its appeal. If I have a topic I know will take more time, planning ahead lets me evaluate where it best fits. Recently, looking at the life of Moses, I knew I wanted to highlight his birth (and adoption), the burning bush, the plagues/Pharaoh, the 10 commandments, and following God into the unknown (by cloud and by fire). I was able to plug right into a month that naturally had 5 Sundays to accommodate the theme—Leading the Lost—without grappling with cutting one to fit or adding to bridge two months.

As you fill in blanks, leave time for review games and even themed movie days. These are a great way to provide closure so you can pivot from one topic to another that is unrelated. The review is not only great for your kids, it provides a way for you and your leaders to observe all that the kids have absorbed. It's motivating!

Did you notice this section began with "fill in (*most of*) the blanks?" You may or may not get every blank filled as you plan the year; that's okay! Pray over those times and ask the Lord for direction. Consider using them to invite in a guest speaker like a missionary or someone who serves in a different ministry to give their testimony. You can use them as a family Sunday or as a service project. Or head back to social media and tap the wealth of resources that exist in your community of fellow kidmin leaders. Even if the plan isn't complete, you're well on your way to a strong, effective year because of what you have in place.

#6: DON'T SWEAT IT WHEN THINGS DON'T GO AS PLANNED

Proverbs 16:9 says, *"We can make our plans, but the Lord determines our steps"* (NLT). Sometimes, plans have to change. Maybe the Lord lays something on your heart that is the heartbeat of your ministry, right then and there, that you couldn't have foreseen nine months earlier when you planned the year. Other times, you're forced to accommodate a change in program, structure, location, or volunteer team that's beyond your control. Whatever the catalyst for change, it's not a bad thing, even if it means scrapping your plan. On the contrary, what an exciting opportunity for the Holy Spirit to fill in the gaps and work mightily in our stead! Lean on Him. He always comes through!

Planning ahead, especially for a whole year, is a lot of work. It takes time and can seem like a daunting task. But when you enter a new year/school year with a plan, you enter it with confidence—not in yourself or in your plan. Rather, you're confident because you've sought the Lord and allowed Him to order your steps. You have cause to be excited as you anticipate how the Lord will work. Don't be afraid to share the plan with others. Sharing it with volunteers shows how invested you are in the ministry and challenges them to be just as invested too. It gives them a chance to go before the Lord in prayer with specific ways the Lord can prepare the hearts they minister to. Sharing the plan with parents gives them time to come up with ways to reinforce what their kids are learning at church from home and the ability to follow up each week regarding the lesson. For the leadership above you, a plan gives them confidence in your calling and your heart for ministry. Lastly, remember the 6-year-old and the tween at the beginning of the chapter? A plan helps prepare them and all the kids in your ministry for spiritual prosperity. It's a plan that heads toward an abundant life filled with the peace that surpasses all understanding, made possible only by life-changing faith in Jesus Christ, who you played a role in leading them to.

You, friend, are stronger when you plan for the year ahead. *"Commit your actions to the Lord and your plans will succeed"* (Proverbs 16:3, NLT).

Kristy Motte is the Elementary Children's Director at the Rock Church of Fenton and teaches for Liberty University, is a mom of three kids ages 1-5, and passionate about serving alongside her husband in family ministry. In her spare time (as if there is such a thing!), she loves good coffee, anything competitive, and exploring someplace new.